The MAILBOX® INSTANT Activities

More than 400 skill builders you can use today!

- ⬡ **Organized by common classroom supplies**
- ⬡ **Little or no preparation needed**
- ⬡ **Great for group and center times**
- ⬡ **Fun for students**
- ⬡ **Perfect for busy teachers**

Looking for a specific skill? See the **Skills Index** on page 142!

Managing Editor: Kimberly Brugger-Murphy

Editorial Team: Margaret Abed, Becky S. Andrews, Randi Austin, Diane Badden, Pamela Ballingall, Brooke Beverly, Janet Boyce, Amy Brinton, Tricia Kylene Brown, Kimberley Bruck, Karen A. Brudnak, Ann Bruehler, Marie E. Cecchini, Andrea Chouhan, Beth Clipp, Pam Crane, Chris Curry, Kathryn Davenport, Roxanne LaBell Dearman, Beth Deki, Lynn Drolet, Sarah Foreman, Pierce Foster, Kristin Bauer Ganoung, Deborah Garmon, Deborah Gibbone, Ada Goren, Heather E. Graley, Karen Guess, Tazmen Hansen, Marsha Heim, Lori Z. Henry, Laura Johnson, Krystle Short Jones, Kelly Kramer, Debra Liverman, Kitty Lowrance, Karen Luba, Brenda Miner, Suzanne Moore, Jennifer Nunn, Tina Petersen, Robyn Pryor, Mark Rainey, Greg D. Rieves, Kelly Robertson, Hope Rodgers, Eliseo De Jesus Santos II, Rebecca Saunders, Betty Silkunas, Donna K. Teal, Rachael Traylor, Sharon M. Tresino, Carole Watkins, Zane Williard

www.themailbox.com

Table of Contents

Classroom Supplies

What's Inside

Activities organized by common classroom supplies

 Craft Sticks

Stick Letters
Forming letters
Give each child several craft sticks. Name a letter that contains only straight lines. Then encourage each student to form the letter with his craft sticks. Repeat the activity with different letters.

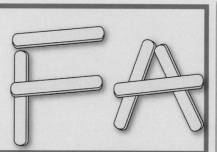

Quick-to-read activities

Digging for Bones
Fine-motor skills
Bury a variety of craft sticks (dinosaur bones) in a tub of sand. A student digs through the sand with a spoon to find a bone. He uses a pair of tweezers to pick up the bone and place it on a tray. Then he brushes the sand residue from the bone using a paintbrush.

It's a Match!
Matching patterns
Use small stickers to program pairs of jumbo craft sticks with matching patterns. A child chooses a craft stick and studies the pattern. Then she finds the craft stick with the matching pattern and places the pair to the side. She continues for each remaining pair of sticks.

Helpful art

Lots of learning for students!
Skills include literacy, math, science, fine motor, and gross motor.

Our Class Wish List

If you are able to donate any of the circled items,
we will be tickled pink!

animal figurines
balls
beanbags
bingo daubers
boxes
building blocks
bulletin board borders
cardboard tubes
carpet squares
catalogs

chalk
clothespins
cookie cutters
cotton balls
counters
craft foam
craft sticks
crayons
crepe paper streamers
dice
die-cut shapes
dominoes
foam letters and numbers
hoops
index cards
jump ropes
lids
linking cubes
magazines
magnetic letters and
    numbers
markers and marker caps

newspaper
paper bags
paper plates
paper towels
pattern blocks
pipe cleaners
plastic eggs
plastic food
play dough
pom-poms
puppets
puzzle pieces
resealable plastic bags
rhythm instruments
rubber stamps
sponges
stencils
sticky dots
sticky notes
tape
toy vehicles
yarn

Thank you!

Dear Family,

We are collecting the following items for upcoming class activities. If you can provide any of these items, we would appreciate it.

Thank you!

Instant Activities • ©The Mailbox® Books • TEC61270

Dear Family,

We are collecting the following items for upcoming class activities. If you can provide any of these items, please send them in by _____,
day

_____.
date

Thank you!

Instant Activities • ©The Mailbox® Books • TEC61270

Animal Figurines

It's a Parade!
Counting
Invite a child to roll a die and count the dots. Then have her count aloud as she places a corresponding number of animals in a line. Continue in the same way, instructing each child to place her animals at the end of the line to create an imaginary parade.

Which Home?
Sorting by habitat
Put a collection of farm, pet, and jungle animals in a container. Set the container near a barn, a house, and a tree cutout. A child removes each animal from the container and places it near a cutout that symbolizes the animal's habitat.

Class Story
Speaking
Write on chart paper the sentence starter shown. Then put a variety of animal figurines in a sack. Invite a volunteer to choose an animal. Then encourage the child to complete the sentence, naming the animal and something that animal might be doing.

One day I was at the park, and I saw...a tiger on the swings with my friend Sam!

A Barn for One
One-to-one correspondence

Provide several barn cutouts along with a container of farm animals. Invite a child to place one animal on each barn, identifying the animals as he goes.

Take a Guess
Participating in a game

Give each child an animal. Invite a volunteer to secretly choose a classmate's animal and then make the animal's sound. Encourage the remaining youngsters to guess the name of the animal and identify which classmate has it in his possession.

Land or Ocean
Categorizing

Provide land and ocean animals along with sheets of brown and blue paper (land and water). Invite a child to pick an animal and describe its characteristics. Then have her place the animal on the appropriate paper to show where it lives.

Does It Belong?

Discriminating by category

Display a set of animals that belong to the same geographic location. Then add one animal that doesn't belong. Challenge a student to find the animal that does not belong and explain his reasoning.

Simple Shapes

Forming shapes

Provide a supply of plastic animals along with several shape outlines, such as a circle, a square, and a triangle. A student chooses a shape; then he places animals along the outline to form the shape.

Hidden Animal

Following oral directions

Secretly hide an animal in your classroom. Then give youngsters oral directions to follow—such as "Hop to the reading area" and "Tiptoe to the easel"—to lead them to the animal's secret hiding place.

Animal Antics

Beginning sounds

Select several animals whose names begin with different sounds. Display an animal and have youngsters say its name and beginning sound. Then have each child move about the room, pretending to be the animal.

Moving Along

Listening

Just prior to a transition, such as lining up to leave the room or washing hands, give each child an animal. Tell youngsters to listen carefully; then signal each child when it is her turn to transition by making her animal's sound.

Colorful Animals

Sorting by color

Provide a container filled with animals in solid colors. For each color, place a coordinating sheet of construction paper near the container. Invite youngsters to sort each animal onto its corresponding paper.

Balls

Rolling Along
Making predictions

Gather an assortment of balls. Then use a board to create a ramp. A youngster chooses two balls. He predicts which ball will roll down the ramp the fastest. Then he rolls each ball down the ramp to test his prediction.

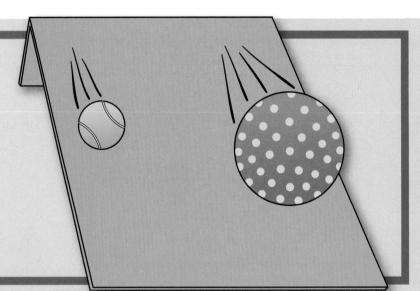

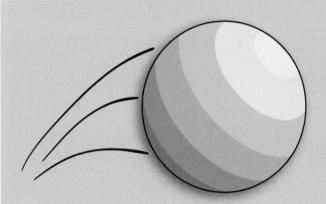

ABC Pass
Alphabet knowledge

Seat youngsters in a circle and hand a child a ball. Have her say, "A," and then pass the ball to a classmate beside her. Have that classmate say, "B," and then pass the ball to the next child. Continue in the same way until the alphabet has been recited.

Roll a Shape
Identifying shapes

Use tape to make a large triangle on the floor. Have youngsters identify the shape. Then invite three students to sit near the corners of the triangle. Have them roll a ball to each other to reinforce the shape.

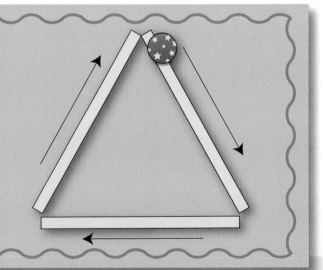

High or Low
Making comparisons
Collect different types of balls. Invite students to drop the balls, in turn, on a hard surface and compare how high they bounce.

Bounce and Tell
Oral language
Arrange youngsters in a circle. Say, "My favorite food is" and then finish the sentence. Bounce the ball to a student and have him complete the prompt. Then have him continue the game by bouncing the ball to a classmate.

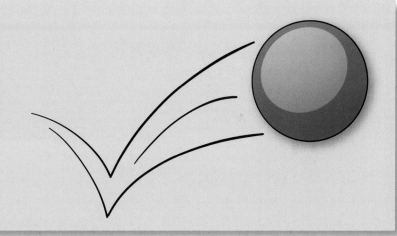

Ping-Pong Transfer
Fine-motor skills
Provide a container of Ping-Pong balls. A child uses a pair of tongs to pick up a Ping-Pong ball and transfer it to an empty container. She continues until all the balls have been transferred.

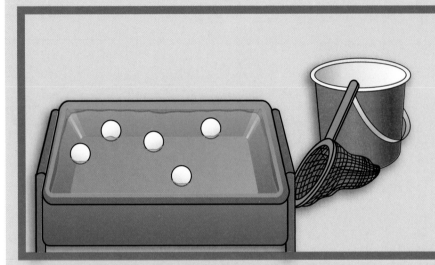

Float and Scoop
Counting

Float a supply of Ping-Pong balls in your water table. Place a plastic pail nearby. Encourage a child to use a small fishnet to scoop up the balls and put them in the pail. Then have him count the balls as he moves them from the pail back into the water.

Golf Balls and Tees
Color matching

Pair golf tees and golf balls. Then use a permanent marker to draw a different color of matching dots on each pair. Press the tees into a large piece of polystyrene foam. A child chooses a golf ball and places it on its matching tee.

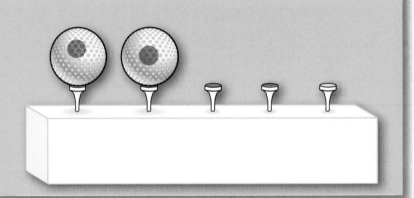

Fill the Jar
Number identification

Provide a large plastic jar and a collection of balls. Place several number cards facedown. Invite a volunteer to turn over a card and identify the number. Then have him count aloud as he puts the corresponding number of balls into the jar.

Dip and Roll
Artistic expression

A child puts a circle cutout in the bottom of a pail. Then she uses a spoon to dip a golf ball in paint and place it in the pail. Have her tilt and move the pail to roll the ball across the paper. Encourage her to continue with other golf balls and colors of paint.

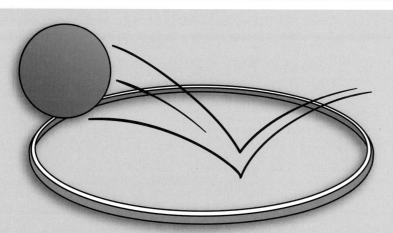

Bounce and Catch
Gross-motor skills

Place a plastic hoop on the ground. Instruct two children to stand outside the hoop facing each other. Encourage the partners to practice bouncing and catching a ball using the inside of the hoop as a target.

The Right Fit
Comparing sizes

Gather a variety of balls in different sizes. Cut in the sides of a box holes that correspond to the sizes of the balls. A child places each ball in the box by inserting it into the correctly sized hole.

Beanbags

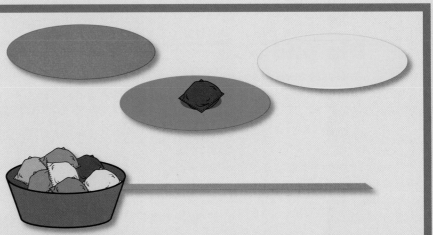

Color Toss
Identifying colors
Place a variety of colorful circle cutouts on the floor. Attach a tape line a few feet from the circles; then set a container of beanbags near the line. A child stands on the line and tosses a beanbag on a circle. Then she identifies the circle's color.

Teacher Says
Recognizing body parts
Give each youngster a beanbag. Then lead the group in playing a body parts awareness game by giving directions such as "Put your beanbag on your shoulder" and "Touch your beanbag to your shin."

Walking Tall
Gross-motor skills
Place number cards in a bag. Invite a child to pick a card from the bag and announce the number. Then place a beanbag on top of her head. Encourage her to walk the corresponding number of steps while balancing the beanbag.

Above or Below

Positional words

Give each child a sheet of construction paper and a beanbag. Then have him place his beanbag, in turn, *on, under, beside, above,* and *below* his paper and then *between* his and a classmate's papers.

Word Toss

Letter-sound association

Announce a letter name and its sound. Next, toss a beanbag to a child. Encourage her to name a word that begins with the sound and then toss the beanbag back to you. Continue in the same way with other letters.

T says /t/.

Flip and Drop

Identifying numbers

Place several number cards facedown near an empty container and a supply of beanbags. Invite a child to flip over a card and identify the number. Then have him count aloud as he drops the corresponding number of beanbags in the container.

Bingo Daubers

Modern Art
Fine-motor skills

Encourage each child to use several colorful bingo daubers to make dots on a sheet of construction paper. Then prompt her to use a variety of markers to connect the dots. The result is a lovely and unique piece of modern art!

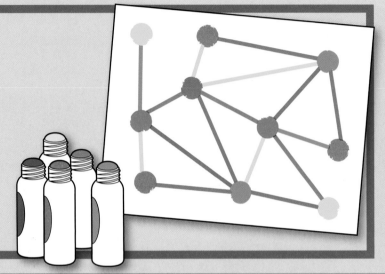

C Is for Caterpillar
Forming the letter C

Give a child a sheet of construction paper labeled with the letter C. Have her trace the letter with her finger and say its name. Explain that the word *caterpillar* begins with the letter C. Then have the youngster use a bingo dauber to make dots on the letter so they resemble a caterpillar. When the ink is dry, encourage her to add details with a fine-tip marker.

Red, Yellow, Red, Yellow
Duplicating and extending patterns

Use bingo daubers to program two or three construction paper strips with simple patterns. Ask a youngster to choose a strip and use a bingo dauber to copy the pattern on a blank paper strip. For an added challenge, have her extend the pattern onto a second paper strip.

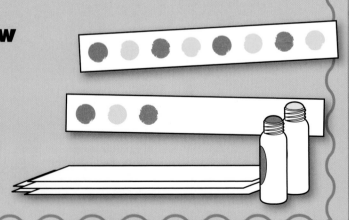

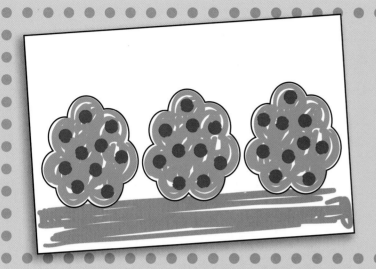

Blueberry Bushes
Making sets of ten
Draw three large blueberry bushes on a sheet of construction paper. A child colors the bushes and then uses a blue bingo dauber to make ten berries on each bush. After the ink dries, he counts each set of berries aloud and adds any desired details to his artwork.

Spiffy Scales
Investigating living things
Show students pictures of fish with clearly visible fish scales. (If desired, have students compare the pictures of fish to pictures of animals that have fur or feathers.) Next, give each child a fish cutout and have her use bingo daubers to make overlapping prints, as shown, so they resemble scales.

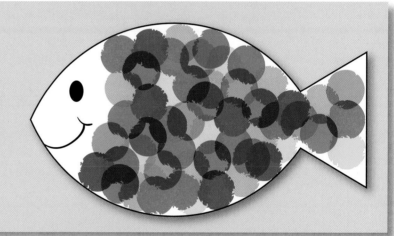

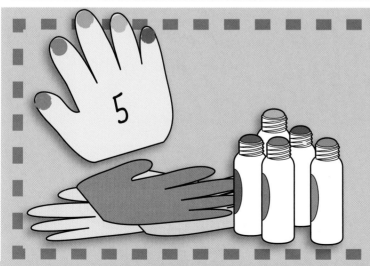

Fancy Fingernails
Identifying numbers, counting
Label hand cutouts with different numbers and attach them to a sheet of chart paper. Have a child name the number on a hand and then use a bingo dauber to "paint" the corresponding number of fingernails. Continue until each number has been identified.

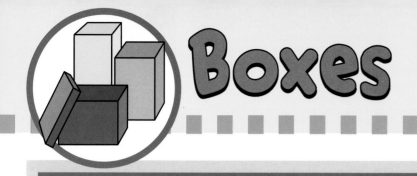

Boxes

Orderly Fashion

Ordering by size

Provide a collection of different-size boxes that are similar in shape. Instruct a child to order the boxes from smallest to largest. Then encourage her to mix the boxes and order them from largest to smallest.

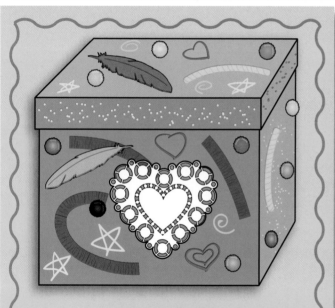

Stunning Craftsmanship

Art

Gather a supply of boxes in different shapes and sizes and provide an assortment of collage materials. Encourage each child to explore his creativity by decorating a box using materials of his choice.

Tall Tower

Hand-eye coordination

Place a supply of boxes in a large open area. Challenge little ones to build a tower by stacking as many boxes as they can without making them fall.

Gorgeous Gift Wrap

Visual discrimination

Wrap each of several identical lidded boxes with different patterns of gift wrap. Place the lids and boxes in two separate piles. A youngster attaches the lids to the matching boxes.

Toy Boxes
Comparing sizes

Provide several different-size boxes along with toys that correspond to each box size. A youngster arranges the boxes and then the toys in order from largest to smallest. Then she places a toy in each box.

Knock 'em Down!
Gross-motor skills

Stand empty food boxes in a row. Mark a start line several feet from the boxes. Then invite a youngster to throw a beanbag at each box to knock it down.

Available Space

Spatial awareness

Give a child a sheet of construction paper and a supply of blocks. Invite her to build a structure, challenging her to keep the entire structure on the sheet of paper.

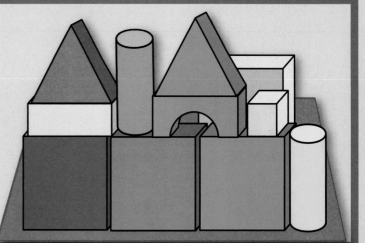

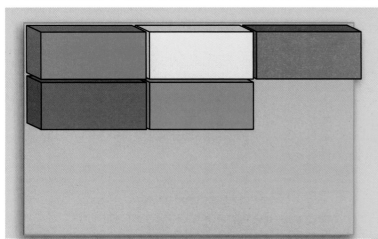

Guess How Many

Estimating

Give a child a large sheet of construction paper. Ask her to estimate how many blocks will be needed to cover the paper. After she makes her guess, have her count aloud as she covers the paper with blocks. Then have her compare her estimate to the actual number of blocks.

Out of Sight

Visual memory skills

Randomly place blocks on the floor, making sure each one has a match, and cover each block with a sheet of paper. In turn, have each child uncover two blocks. If the blocks match, he places them to the side. If they do not match, he re-covers them. Play continues until all the blocks have been matched.

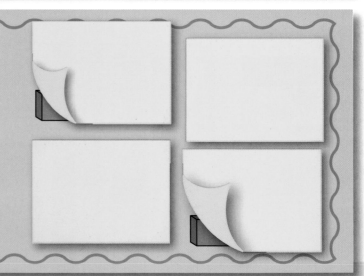

Copycat Structure

Visual discrimination

Give a pair of students identical sets of blocks. Have one child use her blocks to build a structure. Then challenge her partner to duplicate the structure. Encourage students to switch roles and repeat the activity.

Cleanup Crew

Building cooperation skills

Have youngsters put away blocks with this cooperative activity. Encourage a few students to form a line. Prompt the child at one end of the line to pick up a block. Then have students pass the block from classmate to classmate until it is placed back on its shelf.

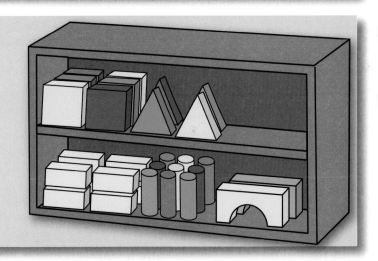

Favorite Flavor

Graphing

Place three sheets of paper on the floor to represent ice cream flavors. Have each youngster place a block on a sheet of paper to show his preferred flavor. Then lead youngsters in counting the blocks and comparing the results.

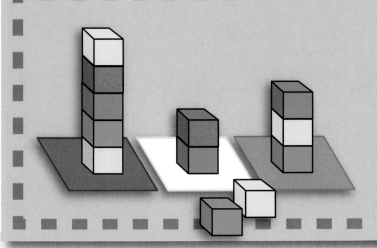

Bulletin Board Borders

Patterning Practice

Extending a pattern

Cut apart the images on decorative bulletin board border to make a supply of patterning pieces. Encourage a child to arrange the pieces on a flat surface to make simple patterns.

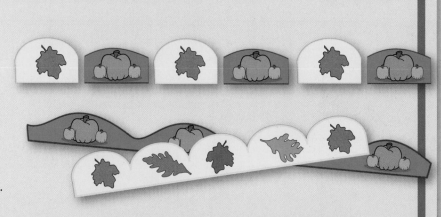

Ridged Designs

Prewriting skills

Place ridged border scraps at a table. A child places a sheet of paper on top of a border; then she rubs the side of an unwrapped crayon over the paper. She repeats the process with different colors to create a masterpiece.

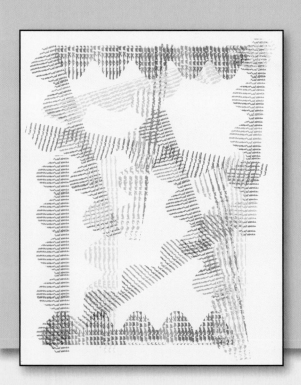

Between the Ridges

Cutting skills

Provide scissors and a supply of ridged bulletin board border scraps. Invite youngsters to practice their cutting skills by cutting the border between the ridges. When students are done, simply add the remnants to your collage box.

Just Right!
Matching lengths
Provide several objects of different lengths. Then cut a strip of border to match the length of each object. A child matches each strip to the corresponding object.

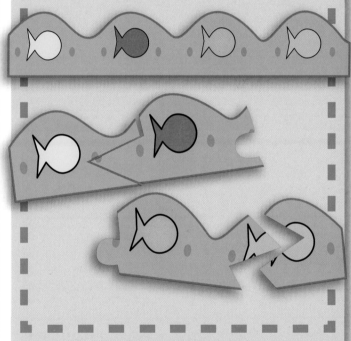

Puzzling Border
Visual discrimination
Cut from decorative border two identical strips; then puzzle-cut one strip into several pieces. Invite a youngster to put the border puzzle together using the uncut strip as a guide.

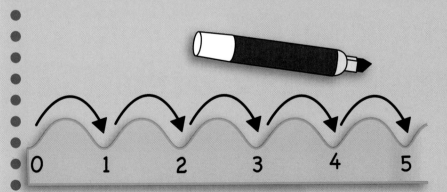

Over the Hills
Counting in number order
Make a simple number line by labeling a length of border with numbers as shown. Prompt a youngster to glide her finger over each hill as she counts aloud.

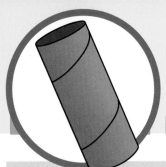

Cardboard Tubes

Familiar Faces
Pretend play
Attach a full-length photo cutout of each child to a separate small cardboard tube. Then place the resulting props in your block area. Youngsters use the props to enhance their block play.

Pass It Along
Hand-eye coordination
Seat students in a circle and give each child a cardboard tube. Demonstrate how to cover one end of the tube with your hand. Place a pom-pom in the open end of the tube and then transfer the pom-pom to the tube of a child next to you. Encourage each child to transfer the pom-pom in the same way to move it around the circle.

Log Jump
Gross-motor skills
Attach large cardboard tubes to your floor as shown so they resemble logs. Encourage students to pretend they are frogs and jump over the logs.

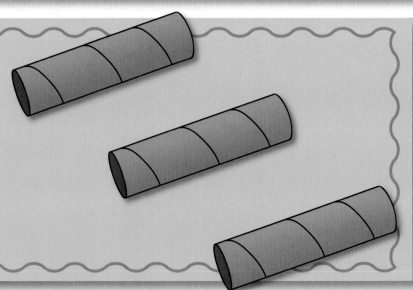

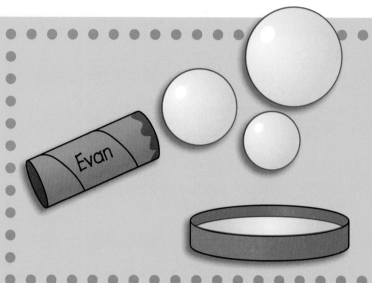

Bubbles, Bubbles
Investigating cause and effect
Fill a shallow container with bubble solution and give each child a cardboard tube labeled with his name. Invite each child to dip one end of his tube into the solution and then blow through the opposite end to make bubbles.

Scoop and Pour
Counting and comparing
Trim cardboard tubes to different lengths. Then stand the tubes in rice in your sensory table and provide several small scoops. Have a child count aloud the number of scoops of rice it takes to fill a tube. Encourage her to repeat the process with a different-size tube; then have her compare the number of scoops needed to fill each one.

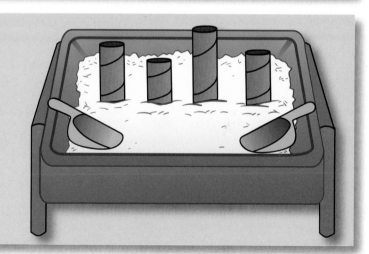

Totally Tubular
Art
Place at a table several shallow containers of paint. A child dips one end of a cardboard tube in paint and then presses it on a sheet of paper. He repeats the process with different tubes and paint colors.

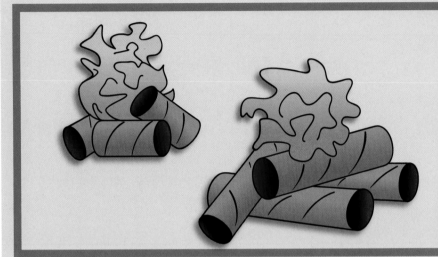

Cozy Campfires
Sorting by size
Provide a supply of long and short cardboard tubes (logs). Students sort the logs into two piles. Then they place crumpled orange tissue paper atop each pile so it resembles a campfire. Have students use the campfires during pretend play.

Whisper Tubes
Oral language
Gather youngsters in a circle and give each child a tube. Place a tube against the ear of the child next to you and whisper a short phrase into the tube. Have that child repeat the phrase in the same manner to his neighbor. Continue until each child has had a turn; then have the last child announce the phrase to the group.

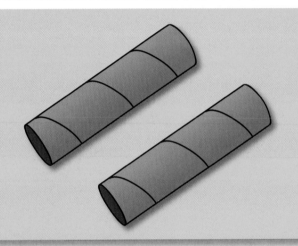

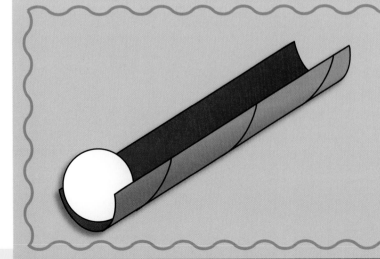

Ping-Pong Chute
Investigating motion
Cut paper towel tubes in half lengthwise to make chutes. Give each child a chute and a Ping-Pong ball. Have her place one end of the chute on the floor and then roll the ball down the chute. Encourage her to repeat the activity, raising and lowering one end of her chute to see how it affects the ball's speed.

Cardboard Tubes

Short and Long

Ordering by size

Cut cardboard tubes in graduated sizes. Challenge a child to arrange the tubes in size order from shortest to longest. Then encourage her to mix up the tubes and arrange them from longest to shortest.

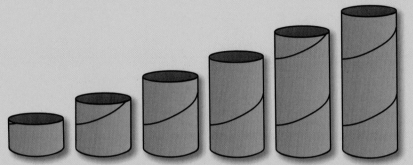

Give It a Shake

Auditory discrimination

Collect a variety of objects such as beans, rice, and bells. Use the objects and heavy-duty tape to make pairs of tube shakers. A student shakes the tube shakers and arranges them in pairs to show the matching sounds.

Rhythm Tubes

Creative movement

Give each child a cardboard tube with crepe paper streamers attached to one end. Play a recording of music with a variety of tempos and encourage each child to move creatively to the music.

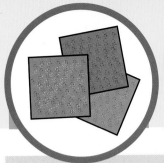

Carpet Squares

Stepping Stones
Gross-motor skills

Arrange carpet squares in a meandering path around the room. Have youngsters pretend the floor is a pond and the carpet squares are large stones. Then direct students to perform gross-motor movement to safely cross the pond.

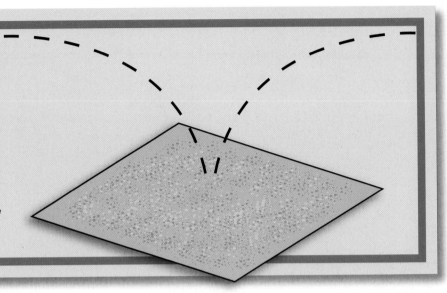

Giant Floor Puzzle
Visual discrimination

Draw simple pictures, such as the one shown, that illustrate carpet squares in different arrangements. Place the pictures near a supply of carpet squares. A child chooses a picture and then arranges the carpet squares to match it.

Listen and Do
Following oral directions

Have each child stand on a carpet square. Then have youngsters follow directions based on the colors of the squares. For example, you might say, "If you are standing on a blue carpet square, jump up and down five times."

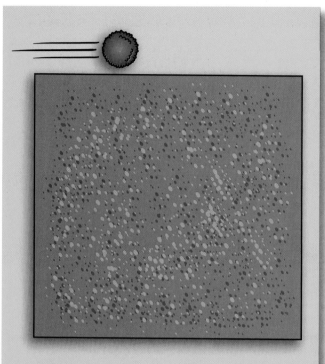

Ladybugs on the Move
Understanding positional words

Give each child a carpet square and a red pom-pom (ladybug). Then lead youngsters in some creeping, crawling fun by directing each child to make her ladybug crawl above, below, beside, under, and around the square.

Imaginary Journey
Contributing to a class story

Sit on a carpet square and say, "One day while I was walking, I found the most incredible carpet square! I sat on it and…" Stand and then invite a child to sit on the square and add to the story. Continue with each remaining child.

Puddle Walkers
Sequencing numbers

Use packing tape to attach a number card from 1 to 10 to each of ten carpet squares (puddles). Invite a student to line up the puddles in numerical order. Then encourage her to walk from puddle to puddle, counting aloud as she goes.

Catalogs

Summer ☀	Winter ❄

Seasonal Wear

Categorizing by season

Make a chart similar to the one shown. Have students look through catalogs and cut out pictures of clothing that would be worn during summer and winter. Have youngsters glue the pictures to the chart.

Handmade Puzzles

Visual discrimination

Glue full-page pictures torn from catalogs onto separate sheets of tagboard. Puzzle-cut each picture and store its pieces in a resealable plastic bag. A child chooses a bag, removes the pieces, and then assembles the puzzle.

Pictures and Words

Creating a rebus sentence

Provide pictures of familiar objects cut from catalogs. Have a child choose a picture and make up a sentence that includes the name of the object. Then record her words on a paper strip and have her glue the picture to the strip in the appropriate location.

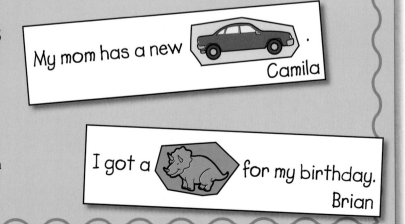

My mom has a new [car].
Camila

I got a [triceratops] for my birthday.
Brian

Catalog I Spy
Observation skills

Glue to a large sheet of paper an assortment of pictures cut from catalogs. Hang the paper on a wall. Then use the masterpiece to play a game of I Spy with your little ones.

Colorful Pictures
Identifying colors

Place three different-colored sheets of paper on the floor. Trim coordinating pictures from catalogs and place them in a bag. In turn, invite each youngster to choose a picture from the bag, identify its color, and then place it on the appropriate paper.

I like this toy because she looks just like my doll at home.

Tracy

I Like It!
Responding to a prompt

Give each child a sheet of paper with the prompt shown. Invite her to look through a toy catalog and cut out a picture of something she enjoys. Then have her glue the picture to her paper and dictate information to complete the prompt.

Chairs

Toys Everywhere
Positional words

Place a chair in your large-group area. Then put toys *on*, *beside*, *under*, *behind*, and *in front of* the chair. Ask a child to choose a toy and tell you where it is in relation to the chair.

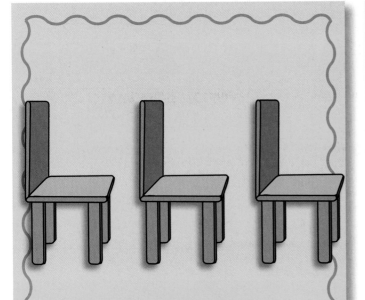

All Aboard!
Ordinal numbers

Place chairs in a row so they resemble the seats on a train. Pretend to be the conductor and use ordinal numbers to direct students to sit in the chairs. Sing the traditional song "Down by the Station." Then have each student exit the train as you call his ordinal number.

Find a Seat
Letter-sound association

Provide six objects with different beginning sounds. Then place five chairs in a row and attach a corresponding letter card to each chair. A child chooses an object, identifies it, and says its beginning sound. Then she places the object on the chair with the matching letter card.

Musical Names

Identifying names in print

Arrange a class supply of chairs in a circle and place a name card beneath each chair. Play upbeat music and have youngsters walk around the chairs. Stop the music and instruct each child to sit in a chair and remove the card from under her seat. Then ask a student to identify the name on her card and locate the appropriate classmate.

Giddyap, Horsey!

Counting

Have each child straddle a chair backward and pretend it is a horse. Announce a number. As youngsters count to the designated number, have them bounce slightly as if they were riding horses. Have students say, "Whoa, horsey!" when they reach the designated number. Then announce a new number and begin another round.

Rolling Along

Participating in a game

Arrange chairs in a line and have each child sit on a chair. Then hand a small ball to the first child in the line. On your signal, have the child roll the ball under his chair to the child sitting behind him. The second child catches the ball and then rolls it in the same manner to the child behind her. Play continues until the ball reaches the last child.

 Chalk

Toss and Hop
Identifying numbers
Use sidewalk chalk to draw an oversize number line on a paved surface. A child stands near the beginning of the number line and tosses a beanbag toward the opposite end. She counts aloud as she hops along the line to reach the beanbag.

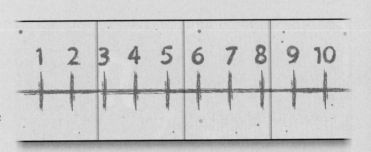

Shapely Workout
Gross-motor skills
Using sidewalk chalk, draw large shapes on a paved surface. Then give youngsters a gross-motor workout and reinforce shape recognition by giving directions such as "Jump around the outside of a square," "Hop to a triangle," or "Tiptoe across a circle."

Chalky Salt
Fine-motor skills
Pour table salt in separate resealable plastic bags and put a piece of colored chalk in each bag. Seal the bags. Then have youngsters manipulate the bags to tint the salt. Have students use the salt for arts-and-crafts projects.

Nifty Names
Writing skills
Use chalk to write each child's name on a separate sheet of black construction paper. Then encourage him to trace his name several times using different colors of chalk.

Bits and Pieces
Artistic expression
Crush colorful chalk remnants in a resealable plastic bag. Place the chalk at a table along with glue and a plastic spoon. A child spreads glue onto a sheet of construction paper and then uses the spoon to sprinkle crushed chalk onto the glue.

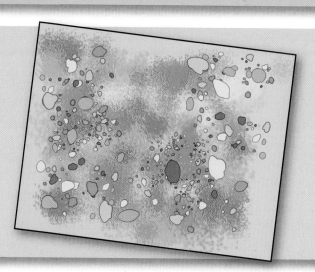

Chalk Review
Forming letters
Before youngsters leave for outdoor play, give each child a piece of sidewalk chalk and announce a letter name. Once outside, each child writes the letter on the pavement. Then he returns his chalk to you before he begins to play.

Clothespins

Spectacular Spiders
Counting

Draw two eyes and a mouth on the backs of several colorful paper plates. A child counts and attaches eight spring-style clothespins to each plate so it resembles a spider.

Clip and Pass

Fine-motor skills

Divide your class into several groups and have each group stand in a row. Give each child a spring-style clothespin; then hand a plastic cup to the first child in each row. On your signal, she uses her clothespin to pass the cup to the next child. Youngsters continue passing the cup down the row using only their clothspins.

Clip, Clip, Repeat
Duplicating a pattern

Program tagboard strips with simple dot patterns and provide a supply of coordinating spring-style clothespins. A youngster chooses a pattern and then clips clothespins to the strip to copy the pattern.

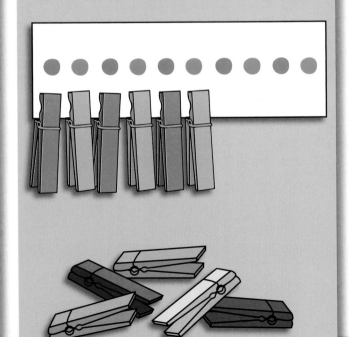

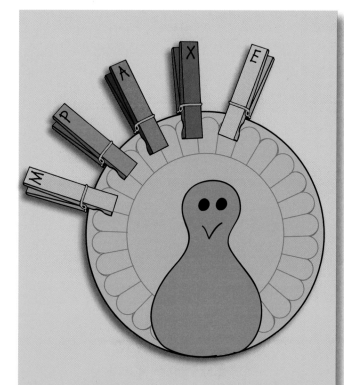

Pretty Peacock

Identifying letters

Attach a simple peacock body to a paper plate. Place the peacock near a supply of clothespins labeled with letters. A child chooses a clothespin, identifies the letter, and attaches it to the peacock.

Grasp and Release

Fine-motor skills

Add a variety of items to a shallow tub of water. A child uses a clothespin to transfer the items from the tub to an empty container.

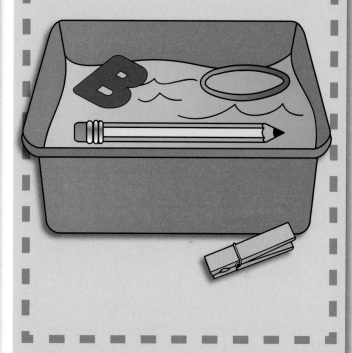

Just Hanging Around

Sequencing numbers

Label ten die-cut shapes with numbers from 1 to 10. Place the shapes near a string suspended between two chairs. A child uses clothespins to attach the die-cuts to the string in number order.

Cookie Cutters

Sandy Words
Identifying letters

Fill a tray with a thick layer of moistened sand. Provide simple word cards and alphabet cookie cutters. A student selects a card, identifies the letters in the word, and presses cookie cutters in the sand to form the word. Then she removes each cookie cutter to reveal the sandy word.

Cookie Cutter Caper
Visual memory

Display several cookie cutters and have students identify the shapes. Then conceal them under a piece of cloth. Secretly remove a cookie cutter before whisking away the cloth. Encourage youngsters to name the missing cookie cutter.

Smallest to Largest
Ordering by size

Provide several identical cookie cutters in graduated sizes. Encourage a child to arrange the cookie cutters in a row from smallest to largest and then from largest to smallest. Finally, have him arrange the cookie cutters in a nesting fashion.

Trace and Match

Visual discrimination

Trace cookie cutters on a sheet of poster board and place the cookie cutters in a container. A student places each cookie cutter on its matching outline.

Blowing Bubbles

Oral-motor skills

Set out a shallow container of bubble solution and a collection of plastic cookie cutters. Invite each child to dip a cookie cutter in the bubble solution and then gently blow through it to produce bubbles.

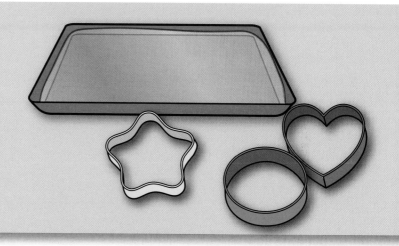

Yummy Shapes

Fine-motor skills

Help each youngster make a simple sandwich. Then have her choose a cookie cutter and press it through the sandwich. Finally, invite her to nibble on her shapely treat.

Printing Press
Identifying numbers, making sets

Place at a table a supply of paper strips labeled with numbers. A student chooses a strip and identifies the number. Then he presses a cookie cutter on an ink pad and makes the appropriate number of prints on the strip.

Cookie Factory
Dramatic play

Stock your dramatic-play area with cookie cutters and a variety of other items used for baking cookies, such as cookie sheets, bowls, utensils, aprons, and oven mitts. Then invite your little bakers to use the props to engage in pretend cookie-making play.

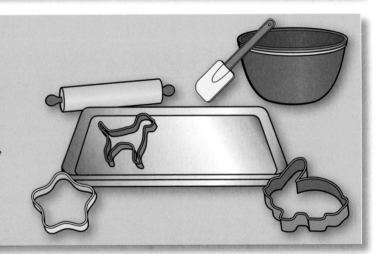

Bag o' Cookie Cutters
Sorting

Gather different sets of cookie cutters, such as letters, numbers, and shapes. Place one cookie cutter from each set on a separate sheet of paper. Then put the remaining cookie cutters in a bag. Invite each child to pick a cookie cutter from the bag and place it on the paper with the corresponding set.

Cookie Cutters

Amazing Mural

Cooperating

Attach bulletin board paper to a tabletop. Invite small groups of students to press cookie cutters on ink pads and then on the paper. Encourage youngsters to color the resulting shapes to make a mural.

Cookie Cutter Clues

Critical-thinking skills

Display several cookie cutters and have youngsters identify each shape. Then secretly choose a cookie cutter and give youngsters a clue to help them identify it. Provide clues as needed until the correct shape is named.

Cutting-Edge Collage

Fine-motor skills

Encourage little ones to trace simple cookie cutter shapes on construction paper. Then help them cut out the shapes. At a later time, have youngsters use the cutouts to make creative collages.

Cotton Balls

Let It Snow!
Engaging in pretend play

Add to your block area a supply of white cotton balls. Students use the cotton balls to create a snowy landscape around their structures.

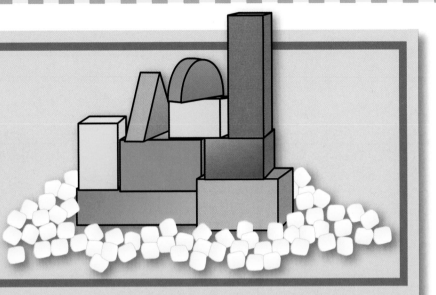

My cloud looks like a fluffy rabbit!

Christina

It Looks Like...
Writing

Have each child glue cotton balls to a sheet of blue construction paper to create a cloud in a specific shape. Then have her dictate or write words to describe her cloud.

Sleepy Sheep
Developing pre-addition skills

Give each child a sheet of red construction paper (barn) and ten white cotton balls (sheep). Next, give youngsters directions for putting groups of sheep in their barns. For example, say, "Two sleepy sheep walked into the barn." Then say, "Three more sleepy sheep walked into the barn." Finally, have youngsters count aloud to determine the total number of sheep in the barn.

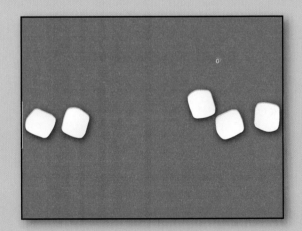

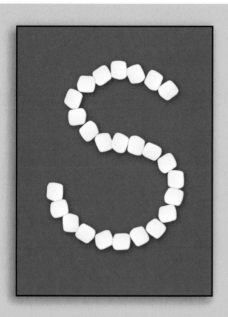

Soft and Fluffy
Forming letters
Give each child a large letter card. Then have him trace the letter with his finger and say its name. Encourage him to glue cotton balls along the letter. After the glue is dry, have him trace the letter again, noting its terrific texture.

Squeezable Fun!
Exploring through the sense of touch
Invite youngsters to explore the texture of a tub of cotton balls. Next, apply nonmentholated shaving cream to the cotton balls. Then invite students to explore the cotton balls again, encouraging them to describe the texture.

Tiny Clouds
Fine-motor skills
Instruct a child to dip a cotton ball (tiny cloud) in a container of water and then squeeze it over an empty cup to collect the raindrops. Encourage her to repeat the process several times; then have her check the cup to see how much rain she has collected.

Counters

Bear's Path
Segmenting words

Have each child place a bear counter and a disposable cup (cave) at opposite ends of a paper strip (path) segmented as shown. Say a word and have youngsters move their bears one space on the path for each word part. Continue until the bears reach the caves.

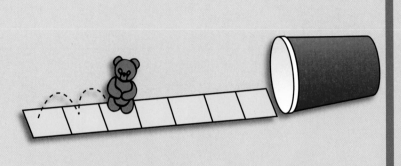

Schools of Fish
Making equal sets

Provide a bowl with an even number of fish counters and give each of two children a blue paper ocean cutout. Have the students take turns removing fish and placing them on their oceans. Then have each student count his fish aloud to verify that both children have equal amounts.

Balancing Act
Understanding ordinal positions

Ask a youngster to line up five bear counters near a rectangular block (balance beam). Then give ordinal directions, such as "Make the second bear walk across the balance beam." After the child completes the task, he returns the bear to its spot. Repeat the process with other directions.

Flip It!
Following directions

Designate a different action to correspond to each side of a two-sided counter, such as "hop three times" for yellow and "bark like a dog" for red. Then flip the counter and encourage youngsters to perform the corresponding motion or make the corresponding sound. After a few flips, designate new directions.

Bedtime Bears
Presubtraction skills

Have each child lay ten bear counters on a felt square (bed). Then lead youngsters in singing the traditional song "Ten in the Bed," directing students to roll each bear out of the bed when indicated.

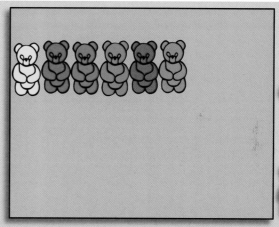

Grab and Count
Comparing sets

Have each of two children take a handful of counters and place them on a tray. Have each youngster count his counters and then compare the two sets using the words *more, fewer,* and *equal.*

Craft Foam

Shapely Rubbings
Fine-motor skills
Attach self-adhesive craft foam shapes to several trays. A student places a sheet of paper in a tray. Then he rubs the side of an unwrapped crayon over the paper to reveal the shapes.

Let's Go Fishing!
Identifying shapes
Attach jumbo paper clips to craft foam shapes. Float the shapes in a water table and provide magnetic fishing poles. A youngster uses a pole to catch a shape. Then she identifies the shape.

Fashionable Headwear
Patterning
Help a youngster attach self-adhesive craft foam shapes to a paper strip to make a pattern. When he is finished, size the strip to fit his head and staple it accordingly. Then have him don his patterned headband.

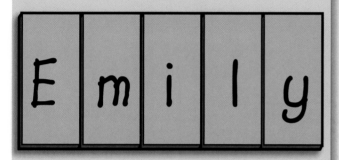

Crafty Names
Identifying letters
Help each child use a permanent marker to write her name on a craft foam strip. Have her cut apart the letters. Then encourage her to reassemble the letters in order, identifying each letter as she works.

Make a Quilt
Identifying colors
Give each child two different-colored squares of craft foam, one slightly smaller than the other. Have a student identify the colors of his craft foam pieces and then place them on the floor in the arrangement shown. Continue with each youngster to form a lovely quilt.

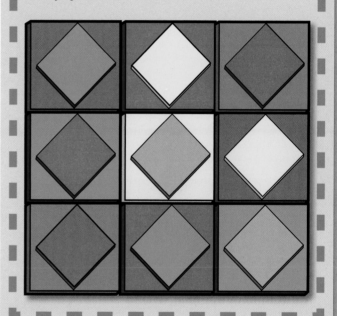

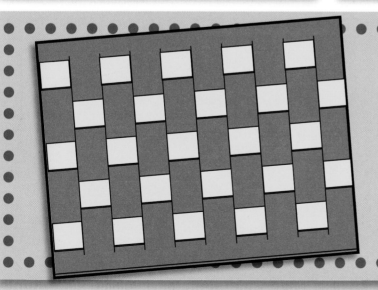

Textured Mat
Fine-motor skills
Fold a sheet of craft foam in half horizontally. Starting at the fold, cut several slits, stopping each slit before reaching the edge. Also cut several craft foam strips. Help a child weave the strips through the slits.

Craft Sticks

Stick Letters
Forming letters

Give each child several craft sticks. Name a letter that contains only straight lines. Then encourage each student to form the letter with his craft sticks. Repeat the activity with different letters.

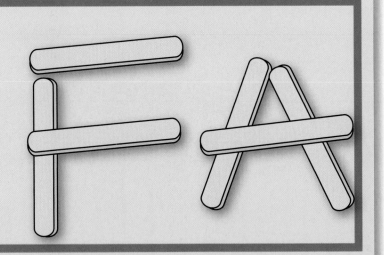

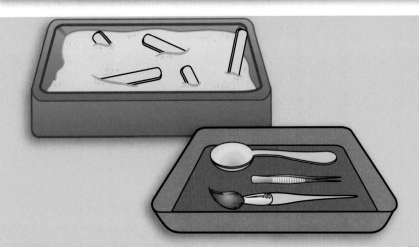

Digging for Bones
Fine-motor skills

Bury a variety of craft sticks (dinosaur bones) in a tub of sand. A student digs through the sand with a spoon to find a bone. He uses a pair of tweezers to pick up the bone and place it on a tray. Then he brushes the sand residue from the bone using a paintbrush.

It's a Match!
Matching patterns

Use small stickers to program pairs of jumbo craft sticks with matching patterns. A child chooses a craft stick and studies the pattern. Then she finds the craft stick with the matching pattern and places the pair to the side. She continues for each remaining pair of sticks.

Count and Match
Matching numbers to sets

Attach a different number of mini pom-poms to each of several craft sticks. Provide corresponding number cards. A child counts the pom-poms on each stick and matches the stick to the appropriate number card.

Measuring Sticks
Nonstandard measurement

A child lies on the floor while a classmate places craft sticks end-to-end beside her body. The students switch places and repeat the process. Then youngsters compare the lengths by the number of craft sticks used.

X Marks the Spot!
Following directions

Attach a craft stick X to a special treat, such as a sheet of stickers or a snack. Then hide the treat in your classroom. Give students directions that lead them to the secret hiding place. Encourage little ones to call out, "X marks the spot!" when the surprise is found. Then have students share the treat.

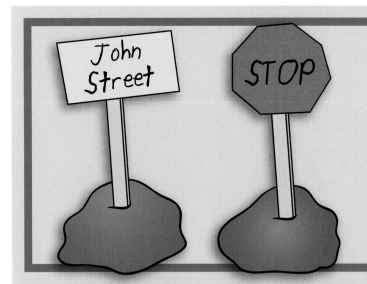

Handmade Signs
Writing

Place craft sticks, paper, scissors, tape, and markers in your block area. Encourage students to use the supplies to create signs to go with their structures. Have them push the signs into balls of play dough to make them self-standing.

Mini Rhythm Sticks
Listening

Provide yourself and each child with a pair of craft sticks. Tap a rhythm with your craft sticks. Then encourage each child to tap his sticks to imitate the rhythm. If desired, challenge a volunteer to tap a simple rhythm for his classmates to follow.

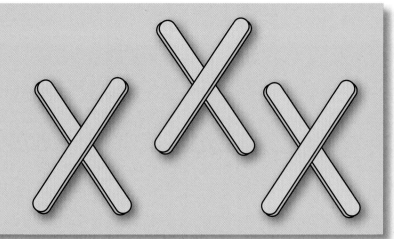

Sandy Shapes
Forming shapes

Provide laminated shape templates, craft sticks, and trays of moistened sand. A child places a shape in a tray. Then she uses a craft stick to trace the shape. Finally, she removes the shape to view her tracing.

Craft Sticks

Pass the Bag
Participating in a group game
Place in a bag craft sticks programmed with directions, such as "Sing the alphabet song," "Hop three times," and "Slither like a snake." Play a recording of music and have students pass the bag around the circle. Periodically stop the music and have the child holding the bag remove a stick. Read the directions aloud for youngsters to follow.

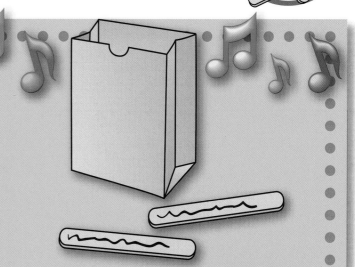

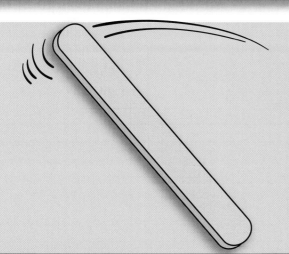

Lead and Prompt
Identifying body parts
Tap a craft stick on your elbow and prompt students to repeat the action with their own craft sticks. Say, "Tap the stick on your…" allowing youngsters to fill in the name of the body part. Repeat the activity with different body parts.

Drop the Sticks
Comparing by quantity
Position two identical box lids as shown. Have a student drop a handful of sticks into the lids. Then have him count aloud the sticks in each lid to determine which lid has more, which lid has fewer, or whether an equal number of sticks fell into each lid.

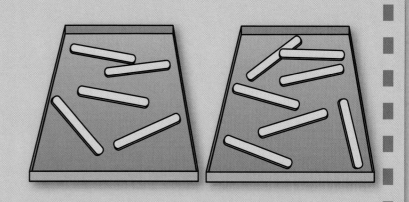

Crayons

What Are the Chances?
Graphing

Make a graph similar to the one shown and place corresponding crayons in a bag. Invite each child to pick a crayon from the bag and color an appropriate space on the graph. After each child has had a turn, have youngsters compare the results.

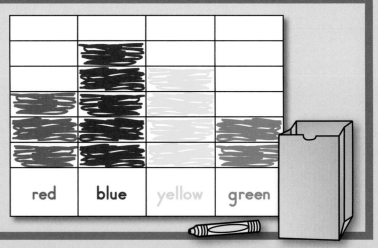

Where Is Yellow Crayon?
Recognizing colors

Give each child several crayons. Then lead youngsters in singing the song shown, directing each child to hold up the designated crayon at the appropriate time. Sing additional verses of the song, substituting another color word where indicated.

(sung to the tune of "Where Is Thumbkin?")

Where is [yellow] crayon?
Where is [yellow] crayon?
Here I am.
Here I am.
[Yellow] is my color—
Such a pretty color.
Yes, indeed!
Yes, indeed!

Marvelous Masterpiece
Fine-motor skills

Give each child a sheet of white construction paper and a black crayon. Have her make a scribble design on the paper. Then encourage her to color the spaces to create a beautiful design.

Beat the Timer
Sorting by color
Label containers with colorful sticky dots. Then provide a supply of crayons in corresponding colors. Set a timer and challenge a small group of students to sort the crayons into the containers before the timer runs out.

What's New?
Visual memory
Display two or three different crayons and have students identify each color. While youngsters close their eyes, add a different crayon to the display. Have little ones open their eyes and then encourage a volunteer to name the color of the crayon that was added.

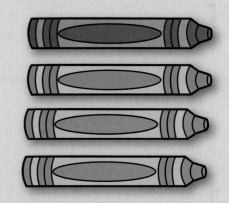

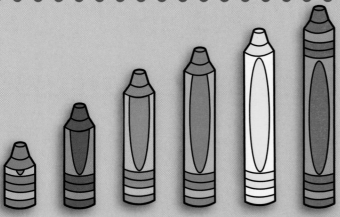

Colorful Row
Ordering by length
Provide several crayons that vary in length. Invite a child to place the crayons from shortest to longest. Then have him scramble the crayons and arrange them from longest to shortest.

Crepe Paper Streamers

Hula Skirts
Patterning

Have each child attach colorful lengths of crepe paper streamers to a paper strip to make a pattern as shown. When the glue is dry, secure each child's strip around her waist. Then play a recording of tropical music and invite youngsters to dance while wearing their patterned hula skirts.

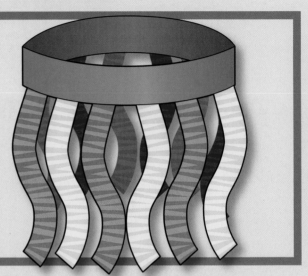

Cross the River
Gross-motor skills

Choose a youngster to stand to one side. Then give the remaining youngsters crepe paper streamers and have them sit on the floor in two rows facing each other. As they wiggle their strips near the floor, prompt the standing youngster to "cross the river" by walking through the streamers. Repeat the process, having students skip, hop, and jog across the river.

Square Dancing
Recognizing numbers

Label four crepe paper streamers with numbers and attach them to your floor to make a square. Play a recording of music and have youngsters dance around the outside of the square. Periodically stop the music and call out a number. Direct each child standing next to the number to repeat an action that number of times, saying, for example, "Clap your hands three times."

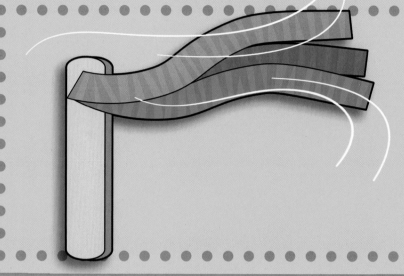

Wind Testers
Investigating wind
Have each student attach crepe paper streamers to a jumbo craft stick to make a wind tester. Then take students outside on a windy day and have them describe what happens when they hold their testers in the air.

Colorful Collages
Art
Provide a supply of streamers. A child cuts pieces from streamers and glues the pieces to a sheet of paper to make a colorful masterpiece.

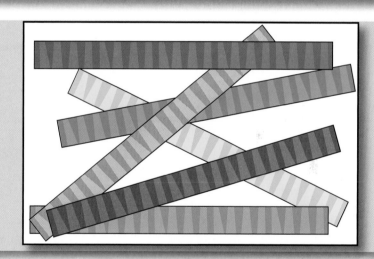

Shorter, Longer, or Equal
Nonstandard measurement
Give each child a crepe paper streamer. Direct him to use his streamer to find objects that are longer than, shorter than, or the same length as his streamer.

Dice

Roll and Count
Counting

Provide one (or two) jumbo die and a collection of items such as seashells, teddy bear counters, or plastic dinosaurs. A child rolls the die and counts aloud the number of dots. Then he counts aloud a corresponding number of items.

Ready for Action!
Following directions

Invite a child to roll a jumbo die and count aloud the number of dots. Then encourage her to announce to her classmates a direction that incorporates the number of dots, such as "Tap your head four times."

All in a Row
Ordering sets

Place six jumbo dice in a basket. Ask a child to remove a die and locate the side that shows one dot. Have him count the dot and then place the die on the floor. Have him repeat the process with the remaining dice, finding each subsequent set in the counting sequence.

Count and Check
Graphing

Have a student roll a jumbo die and count aloud the dots. Then have her record her roll on a graph similar to the one shown. After each youngster has had a turn, have students count and compare the dot sets rolled.

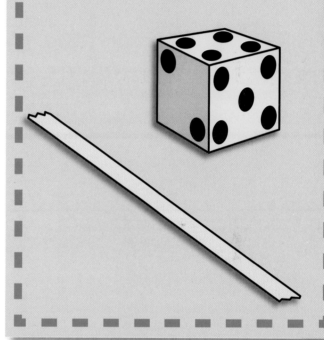

Reaching Our Goal
Gross-motor skills

Instruct little ones to stand in a row parallel to a goal line. Announce a movement, such as galloping. Then roll a die and count aloud the dots. Have each student use the movement to travel toward the goal that number of times.

Lots of Dots
Making identical sets

A child rolls a jumbo die and counts the number of dots. She uses a bingo dauber to make a corresponding dot set on a sheet of paper. Then she circles the set with a marker. She repeats the process several times, circling each set she makes.

Die-Cut Shapes

Tic-Tac-Toe

Participating in a game

Provide a tic-tac-toe board and two sets of five matching seasonal die-cut shapes (game markers). Then encourage students to play a game of seasonal tic-tac-toe.

Hide-and-Seek

Matching sets to numbers

Before students arrive at school, hide die-cut shapes around your classroom. Give a youngster a number card and have him read the number. Then instruct him to collect a matching number of shapes.

Point It Out

Print concepts

Have each child glue a die-cut star to a craft stick. If desired, invite her to decorate the star with glitter. When reading with the child, encourage her to use the pointer to point out known letters, words, and punctuation.

Frog sees a fly.

Storybooks to Share
Writing
Give each child a blank booklet and have her glue one or more die-cut shapes to each page. Prompt her to draw details and write or dictate a sentence about each page.

Listen and Do
Positional words
To play this version of Simon Says, give each child one of several seasonal or themed die-cut shapes. Then announce a shape and a direction using a positional word. For example, say, "If you have a frog, hold the frog over your head."

Outline Art
Fine-motor skills
Die-cut shapes from vinyl placemats. Place the resulting stencils and cutouts at a table. Encourage youngsters to trace the props and color the resulting artwork.

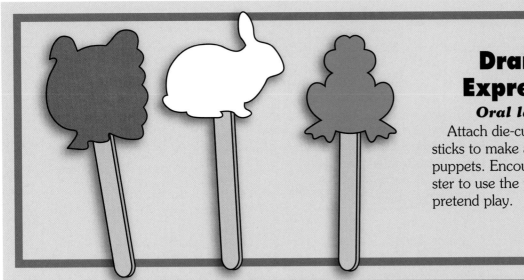

Dramatic Expressions
Oral language
Attach die-cuts to craft sticks to make a variety of stick puppets. Encourage a youngster to use the puppets during pretend play.

Making Groups
Sorting
Give a child a collection of themed die-cut shapes. Have him sort the shapes as desired. Then invite him to explain his sorting rule. Encourage him to sort the die-cuts again using a different rule.

Putting It Together
Spatial sense
Die-cut large shapes from laminated paper. Then puzzle-cut each shape and place the resulting pieces in a resealable plastic bag. Give a bag to a student and have her remove the pieces and put together the puzzle.

Die-Cut Shapes

In a Row
Patterning

Set out paper strips, a variety of die-cut shapes, and glue. Invite a child to choose two or three shapes. Have him arrange the shapes on a strip to make a pattern. After checking his pattern, direct him to glue the shapes in place.

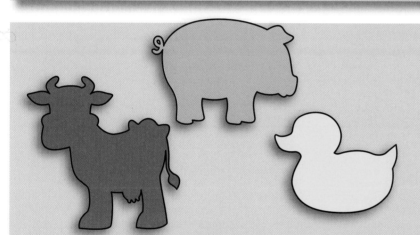

Let Us Tell You
Retelling a story

Prepare a set of die-cut shapes to represent the characters in a story. Give each character to a different youngster and have those students stand. Then guide the seated students to retell the story. During the retelling, have each student holding a character act out that character's part.

Cover It Up
Estimation

Set out a large sheet of construction paper and a supply of like die-cut shapes. Then have each child estimate how many shapes she thinks it will take to cover the paper. Have youngsters count as you place the shapes on the paper. Encourage students to compare their estimates to the actual number of shapes used.

Drop It In
Counting

Number plastic cups from 0 to 12 and place them side by side in order. Set a tub of dominoes nearby. A child chooses a domino and counts the dots on it. Then she drops the domino into the matching cup.

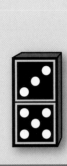

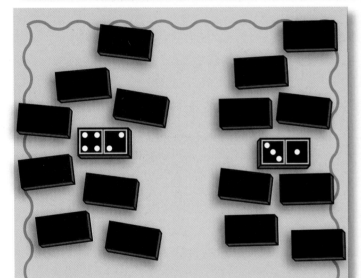

Count and Compare
Comparing sets

For this partner activity, give each child a container of dominoes. Instruct each player to lay his dominoes facedown on a table and set his container nearby. Have each child turn over a domino and count the number of dots. Then have the partners compare the numbers using the words *more*, *less*, or *equal*. Direct each child to place his domino back in his container.

Domino Designs
Making equal sets

Set out a tub of dominoes along with cotton balls and black construction paper. A child takes a domino and counts the number of dots. Then she counts a matching number of cotton balls and glues them to the paper so it resembles the domino.

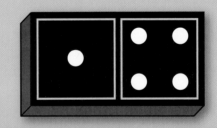

Knock Them Down

Fine-motor skills

Place a tub of dominoes on a hard surface.
Encourage a youngster to carefully stand
several dominoes in a row on their sides and
then tip over the first domino, causing them
all to fall.

Building
Numbers
Forming numbers

Provide extra large number cards and a
supply of dominoes. A child chooses a card and
names the number. Then he places dominoes
on top of the number to form its shape.

Foam Letters and Numbers

Sticky Symbols

Identifying letters and numbers

Float a variety of foam letter and number cutouts in a tub of water. Place a large acrylic picture frame nearby. A youngster chooses a cutout and says its name. Then he places the cutout on the frame. The moisture allows the cutout to stick!

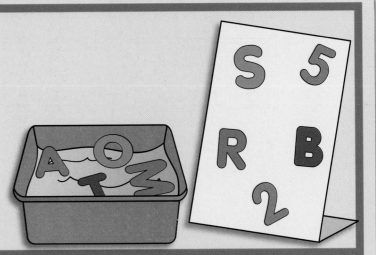

Letters in a Line

Matching letters

Place a tub containing a complete set of foam letters near a strip of adding machine tape labeled with the alphabet. Have two youngsters take turns removing letters from the tub and placing each one below the matching letter on the strip.

Scoop the Soup

Identifying letters

Put a supply of foam letters in your water table. Give a child a slotted spoon and a plastic bowl. Invite her to use the spoon to scoop a serving of alphabet soup into the bowl. Then encourage her to name each letter in her bowl.

Letters	Numbers
I C W	2 5

Letter or Number?
Sorting

Give a child a tub containing foam letters and numbers and a sorting mat labeled as shown. Encourage her to remove each letter or number from the tub and place it on the correct section of the mat.

Shopping Spree
Number recognition, counting

Place a set of foam numbers in a small bag. Invite a child to choose a number from the bag and identify the number. Then give him a basket and encourage him to walk around the room and collect a corresponding number of small objects.

Trace and Draw
Letter-sound association

Invite a child to trace a foam letter cutout onto a sheet of paper. Then encourage her to draw on the paper several objects whose names begin with that letter.

Hoops

Pick and Place
Letter-sound association

Place two hoops on the floor and put a letter card above each hoop. Then set a facedown stack of corresponding picture cards between the hoops. Have each child choose a card, name the picture, and place it in the appropriate hoop.

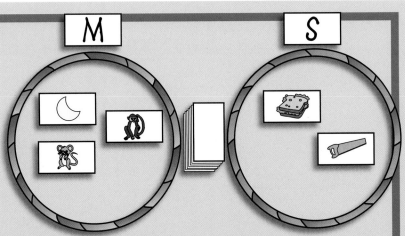

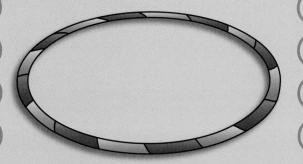

Listen Carefully
Following directions

For this version of Simon Says, place several hoops on the floor and have each child stand next to a hoop. Then announce a direction such as "Put your right foot in your hoop." Continue giving different directions for several more rounds.

Hoop Hop
Counting

Have each child stand in a hoop. Then invite one volunteer to roll a large foam die and count the number of dots. Encourage each child to hop a corresponding number of times in his hoop.

All Kinds of Toys
Classification
Have each child bring a small toy from home. Place a hoop on the floor and have each youngster put his toy outside the hoop. Move a few toys that have a common factor inside the hoop. Then invite students to determine what the toys have in common.

The Colors We Wear
Color identification, comparing sets
Have students stand around a large hoop. Name a color and an article of clothing. Invite any student wearing clothing matching the description to stand in the hoop. Then lead students in comparing the number of students in the hoop with the number outside the hoop.

Who is wearing a green shirt?

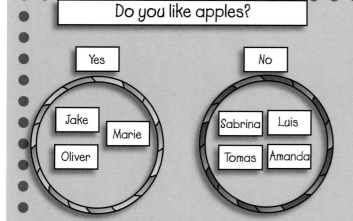

Do you like apples?

Yes

No

Jake
Marie
Oliver

Sabrina
Luis
Tomas
Amanda

Question of the Week
Expressing an opinion
Secure two hoops to a wall and label the hoops as shown. Each Monday, post a yes-or-no question above the hoops. Have each child mount her name card in a hoop to show her answer. Then, each Friday, have youngsters discuss the results.

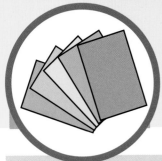

Index Cards

Letters in a Line
Alphabetical order

Fold index cards to make self-standing letter cards as shown. Place the cards in a tub near an alphabet strip. A child removes the cards from the tub. Then she stands the cards in order, using the alphabet strip as a guide.

| A | B | C | D | E | F |

ABCDEFGHIJKLM
NOPQRSTUVWXYZ

Name Scramble
Spelling one's name

Give each child index cards so he has one for each letter in his name. Help him write one letter of his name on each card. Have him shuffle the cards. Then invite him to rearrange the letters to spell his name.

Camping Bears
One-to-one correspondence

Fold a supply of index cards to make mini tents and provide an equal number of bear counters. Have a child count the tents and the bears and then place one bear in each tent.

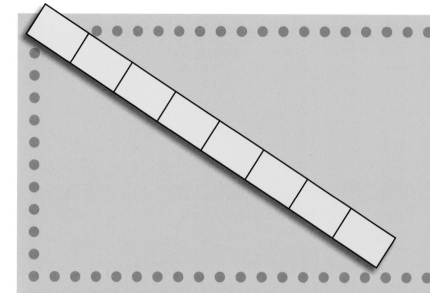

Card Lineup

Estimating, nonstandard measurement

Show students an index card. Then have volunteers estimate how many cards they think can be lined up between two specific points in your classroom. Invite youngsters to help you line up and count the cards. Then have students revisit their estimates.

Hide-and-Seek

Recognizing numbers

Fold index cards to make self-standing number cards as shown. Secretly hide a small object under one of the cards. Then invite a volunteer to name a number and lift the tent to see if the object is there. Continue until the correct tent is chosen.

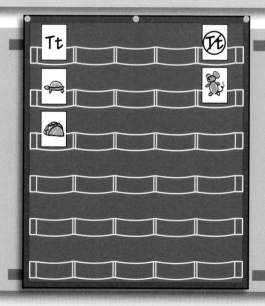

Picture Cards

Beginning sounds

Label index cards with the headings shown and place them in your pocket chart. Encourage half of your class to draw on index cards pictures that begin with the designated letter. Have the remaining students draw pictures that do not. Encourage each child to place his card below the appropriate heading.

Jump Ropes

Match a Rhyme
Rhyming
Arrange pairs of rhyming picture cards on the floor to form a circle. Invite a student to manipulate a jump rope so the ends are pointing to matching rhymes. Have her collect the rhyming cards. Students continue playing until all the matching pairs have been collected.

Student Sort
Sorting
Place a jump rope on the floor to make a dividing line. Designate an attribute for each side of the line, such as light hair and dark hair. Direct each student to stand on the side that is appropriate for him. Then compare the results of the sort.

Snowball Toss
Gross-motor skills
Place a long jump rope on your floor in a straight line. Have each child crumple up a sheet of used white paper to make a snowball. Then have two teams of youngsters stand on opposite sides of the line. At your signal, encourage youngsters to throw their snowballs to the opposite side.

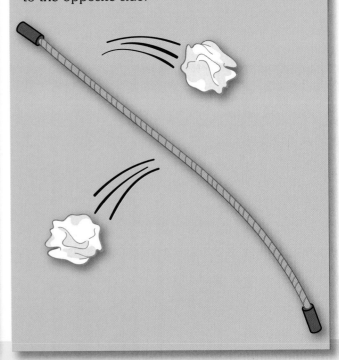

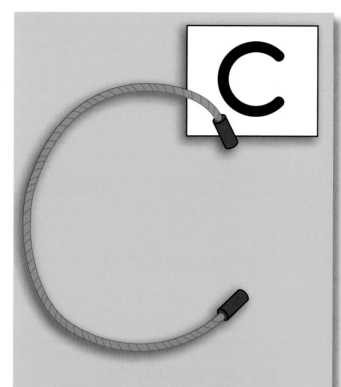

Extra-Large Letters
Forming letters
Set out several jump ropes along with a set of letter cards. Invite a child to choose a letter card. Then have him manipulate one or more jump ropes to form the letter.

Follow the Path
Gross-motor skills
Arrange jump ropes to form a curvy path. Have a child use a desired movement, such as hopping or galloping, to travel the length of the path. Then encourage her to turn around and return along the path using a different movement.

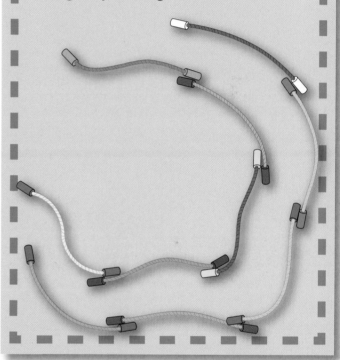

A Spatial Snake
Positional words
Use permanent markers to draw snake facial features on one handle of a jump rope. Place the resulting snake on the floor. Then give a student a direction using a positional word, such as "Jump over the snake" or "Walk beside the snake."

Lids

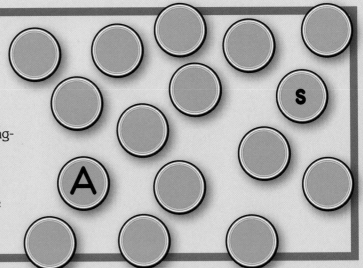

Flip the Lid
Letter matching

Label lids each with an uppercase letter and then label separate lids with the matching lowercase letters. Have two youngsters arrange the lids facedown. Then, in turn, each child turns over two lids. If the lids match, he takes them. If not, he turns them back over. Play continues until all the matches have been found.

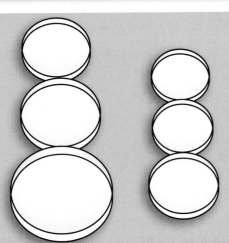

Building Snowpals
Comparing size

Set out a container of white lids (snowballs). Have a youngster arrange the snowballs to make a variety of snowpals in different sizes. Prompt her to compare her snowpals using words such as *small, smaller,* and *largest.*

Pleasing Patterns
Extending a pattern

Use different-colored lids to begin a pattern on the floor. Invite a child to find the next lid needed for the pattern and then place it appropriately. Continue until youngsters have added several lids to the pattern.

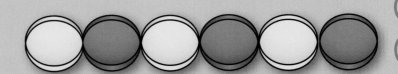

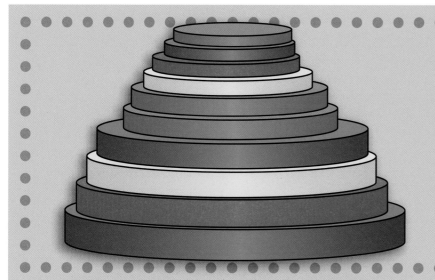

Stack 'em High
Comparing size

Set out a tub containing lids of various shapes and sizes. Invite a youngster to stack the lids to build a tall tower, placing larger lids at the bottom and smaller lids at the top.

It's Abstract!
Art

Have a child place a lid on a sheet of paper and then trace around the lid. Encourage him to make several more tracings on his paper. Then invite him to color his tracings.

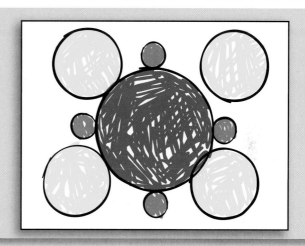

Lid Matchup
Fine-motor skills

Place containers and their corresponding lids in separate tubs. Have a child empty the contents of both tubs. Then encourage him to put each lid on its matching container.

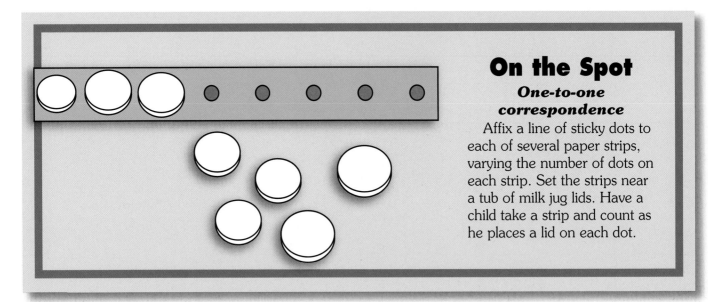

On the Spot
One-to-one correspondence

Affix a line of sticky dots to each of several paper strips, varying the number of dots on each strip. Set the strips near a tub of milk jug lids. Have a child take a strip and count as he places a lid on each dot.

Shapely Stencils
Fine-motor skills

To make a supply of stencils, cut a simple shape in each of several large plastic lids. A child places a stencil on a sheet of paper and uses a crayon to trace the shape.

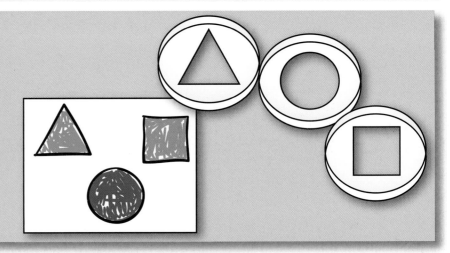

Spell It
Sight words

Place in resealable plastic bags sight word cards and sets of milk jug lids programmed with matching letters. Have a child open a bag and remove its contents. Then prompt him to read the word and arrange the lids to spell the word.

In the Bank

Counting

To make a bank, decorate a coffee can and then cut a large slit in the top. Set the bank near a supply of clean juice can lids (coins). Invite a child to count the coins as he drops them in the bank.

Lid Toss

Gross-motor skills

Place a plastic hoop on the floor and set a tub of lids a few feet away. Invite a child to toss each lid in the hoop. Encourage him to gather the lids and play again.

Orderly Arrangement

Number order

Write each numeral from 1 to 20 on a separate lid and place the lids in a container. A youngster dumps the lids on a work surface and then arranges them in number order, consulting a number line as needed.

| 1 | 2 | 3 | 4 | 5 | 6 | 7 | 8 | 9 | 10 | 11 | 12 | 13 | 14 | 15 | 16 | 17 | 18 | 19 | 20 |

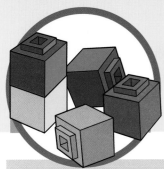# Linking Cubes

Colorful Towers
Sorting, comparing
Invite a child to dump a tub of colorful linking cubes onto a work surface. Have him sort the cubes by color and then link each set. Then have him compare the numbers of cubes in the resulting towers.

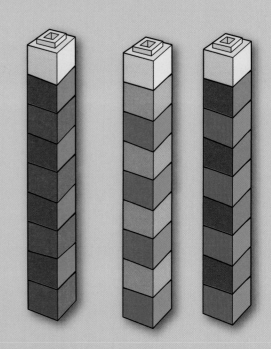

Guess and Count
Estimation
Show a clear tub containing a few cubes. On a personalized sticky note, have each child write an estimate of how many cubes are in the tub. After posting the sticky notes, lead students in counting the cubes. Then encourage them to compare their estimates to the actual number.

Candle Jumping
Creating a pattern
Have each child make a patterned tower (candle) similar to the ones shown. Invite each child to place his candle on the floor. Then lead students in reciting "Jack Be Nimble" and encourage them to jump over their candles when appropriate.

Every Vote Counts
Graphing

Pose a simple question, such as "Do you prefer to eat ice cream in a cone or in a cup?" Tape answer cards to the edge of a table and set a basket of linking cubes next to each choice as shown. Invite each child to cast his vote by adding a cube to the tower that represents his choice.

Count and Connect
Matching sets to numbers

Announce a number and have each youngster link the corresponding number of cubes together to make a tower. When his tower is complete, have him check his work by comparing his tower with another student's tower.

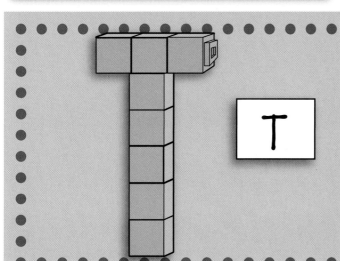

Build a Letter
Recognizing and forming letters

Set out a container of linking cubes and a set of letter cards featuring letters with straight and/or slanted lines. Invite a student to choose a card and name the letter. Then have him use the cubes to form the letter.

Magazines

Cut It Out
Letter-sound association
Program a large sheet of construction paper with a desired letter and review the letter's sound. Then have students cut from magazines pictures of items that begin with the appropriate sound. After you have checked the pictures, have youngsters glue them to the paper.

Our Class
Sharing personal opinions
Have each child draw a self-portrait on a personalized sheet of paper. Then invite him to cut from magazines pictures of things he likes and glue them around his drawing. Bind the pages together with a cover titled "Our Class."

Match It Up
Visual discrimination
Mount large magazine pictures on separate construction paper rectangles and laminate them for durability. Then cut each picture in half and place the halves in a basket. A student removes the halves from the basket and then matches them appropriately.

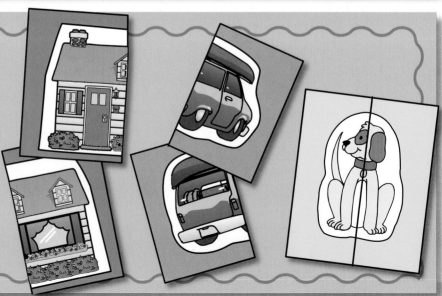

That's Good for Me!
Nutrition

Have each child cut from magazines pictures of healthy foods she likes to eat. Then invite her to glue the pictures to a paper plate. Pair students and encourage the partners to compare and discuss the foods on their plates.

I Spy
Visual discrimination

Write numbers or letters on each of several full-page magazine pictures and then slide each picture into a plastic sheet protector. A child chooses a page and uses a dry-erase marker to circle each number or letter he finds.

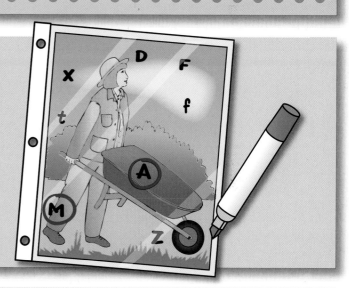

Look and Find
Sight word recognition

Attach a different sight word card to the cover of each of several children's magazines. A child chooses a magazine and reads the word on the cover. Then she looks through the magazine and uses a highlighter to mark the designated word each time it appears.

Magnetic Letters and Numbers

Looking for Letters

Positional words, letter identification

Randomly place several magnetic letters on a magnetic surface. Tell students you are thinking of a letter. Describe the location of the letter using positional words. Then invite a volunteer to point to the letter and say its name.

> This letter is beside the *D.*

Missing Letters

Alphabetical order

On a large magnetic surface, arrange a set of magnetic letters in alphabetical order. Remove a few letters and put them in a small bag. Invite a child to take a letter from the bag and place it in the correct space.

Symbol Sort

Sorting

Use tape to transform a cookie sheet into the sorting mat shown. Provide a tub of magnetic letters and numbers. A child takes a letter or number from the tub. Then he names it and attaches it to the appropriate side of the mat.

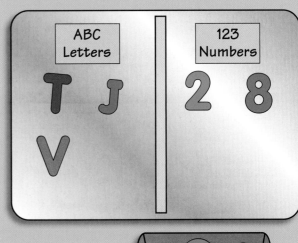

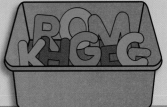

Artistic Numbers
Making sets
Set out a basket of magnetic numbers. A student chooses a number and traces it on a sheet of paper. Then he draws a matching set of objects below the number.

What's Missing?
Visual memory
Arrange magnetic letters and numbers on a board. Review with students the name of each one. Then have students close their eyes. Remove a magnet from the board. Invite youngsters to open their eyes, and encourage a volunteer to name the missing letter or number.

My Name
Spelling one's name
Have a child find the magnetic letters needed to spell her name. Then encourage her to arrange the letters on a flattened piece of play dough. Have her press on the letters and then remove them, revealing the impression of her name.

Markers and Marker Caps

A Colorful Match
Color words, sorting

On each of several large cards write a different color word. Lay the cards out near a small tub of markers. Invite a child to take a marker from the tub and name its color. Then have him place the marker on the matching card. Encourage him to continue until each marker is on the correct card.

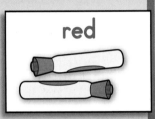

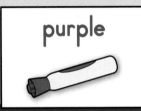

Wonderful Watercolors
Art

Set out paper, dried-out markers, and a cup of water. To make a lovely watercolor picture, invite a youngster to dip the tips of the markers into the water and then draw on his paper.

Act It Out
Dramatic expression

To make a supply of finger puppets, tape character cutouts to separate marker caps. Have a child put a cap on each fingertip and then act out a familiar story or create his own!

Dotty Designs
Fine-motor skills

Set out colorful play dough and several marker caps. Encourage a child to press a cap into the play dough to make lots of dots.

Three in a Row
Participating in a game

On a sheet of paper draw a large tic-tac-toe gameboard. Then have students play a game of tic-tac-toe using two sets of colorful marker caps as game markers.

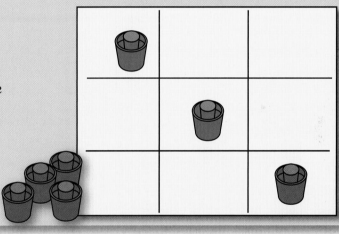

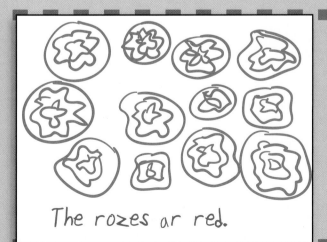

The rozes ar red.

Colorful Expressions
Making connections

Place a class supply of markers in a bag. Give each youngster a sheet of paper and have her take a marker from the bag. Then invite her to draw something associated with that color. Encourage her to dictate or write a sentence about her drawing.

Newspaper

Crumple, Dip, Print!
Fine-motor skills

Have a child crumple a piece of newspaper. Invite him to dip the newspaper ball in a shallow container of paint and then make prints on a sheet of construction paper. Encourage him to repeat the process with other balls of newspaper and different colors of paint.

Detective for a Day
Letter identification

Show a youngster a letter card. Have him identify the letter. Then give him a magnifying glass and encourage him to look at a section of newspaper and find the letter. Whenever he sees the letter, prompt him to mark it with a highlighter.

Tell a Story
Oral language

Give each child a photo clipped from a newspaper and invite him to think about what is happening in the photo. Pair students and encourage one partner to tell a story about his photo while the other child listens. Then have the partners switch roles.

Touch and Find
Writing

Place shredded newspaper in your sensory table. Hide several small objects in the shredded paper. A youngster uses his sense of touch to find an object. Then he draws and labels the object on a sheet of paper.

Clipping Coupons
Fine-motor skills

Gather a large supply of coupon flyers from the newspaper. Invite each child to cut out several coupons and put them in an envelope. Attach a note to the envelope asking parents to encourage their little ones to help with coupon cutting at home.

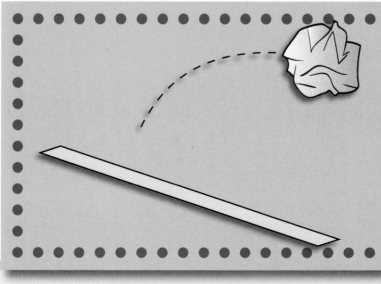

Newspaper Toss
Gross-motor skills

Crumple newspaper to make balls in several different sizes. Attach a tape line to the floor and place the balls nearby. Invite a child to predict which ball will go the farthest when tossed. Have him stand on the line and toss each ball. Then encourage him to evaluate his prediction.

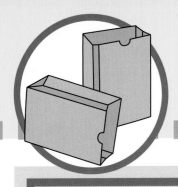

Paper Bags

Bag Bowling

Gross-motor skills, number recognition

Write a numeral from 1 to 10 on each of ten paper lunch bags. Fill each bag with crumpled paper and staple it closed. Arrange the bags like bowling pins and set a small ball nearby. A child rolls the ball toward the bags. Then he names the number on each bag he knocks down.

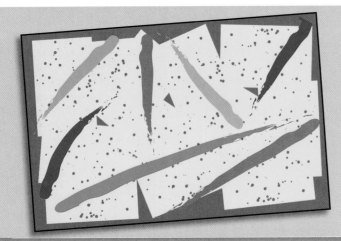

A Unique Masterpiece

Art

Give each child a rectangle cut from a large paper grocery bag. Provide markers, crayons, paint, several different-size paintbrushes, and sponges. A youngster uses the materials to create a unique masterpiece.

Let Me Tell You

Oral language

Give each child a lunch bag and invite her to use craft materials to transform the bag into a puppet that resembles herself. Encourage her to place her puppet on her hand and use it to tell a few things about herself.

Lots of Logs
Spatial skills

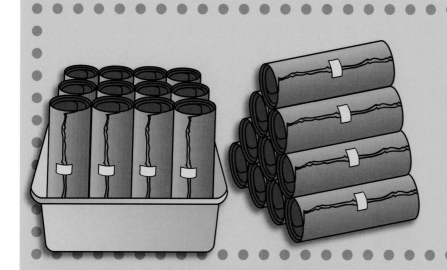

To make logs, roll flattened grocery bags. Then secure each roll with tape. Store the logs on end in a box or tub. Encourage youngsters to use the logs to build a variety of structures.

In the Bag
Letter-sound association

Help each child write an upper-case and lowercase letter pair on a paper lunch bag and then have him decorate his bag. Have him take the bag home and put in it a small object whose name begins with the designated letter. When he returns the bag to school, have him share his object with his classmates.

Wild Hair
Fine-motor skills

Cut a large supply of strips from paper grocery bags. Give each child a white paper circle and several strips. Invite her to draw a face on the circle. Then have her accordion-fold the strips and glue them around the face so they resemble hair.

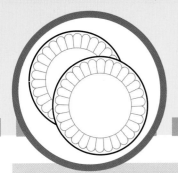

Paper Plates

Find a Match
Matching shapes and colors

Program pairs of paper plates with matching colorful shapes. Scatter the plates facedown. In turn, each partner turns over two plates. If the plates match, then the child removes them. If not, he returns the plates facedown and his turn is over. Play continues until all the matches have been made.

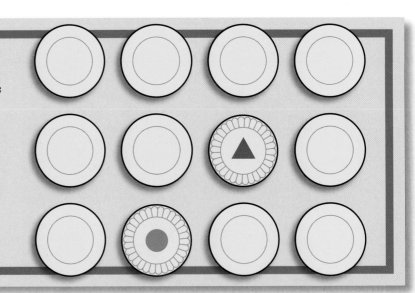

Plate Puzzlers
Spatial skills

Puzzle-cut decorative plates into several pieces. Then place each puzzle in a separate resealable plastic bag. A student chooses a bag and completes the puzzle.

A Snazzy Snowman
Fine-motor skills

To build a snowman, help each child staple three paper plates together as shown. Then encourage him to use markers and paper scraps to decorate the snowman.

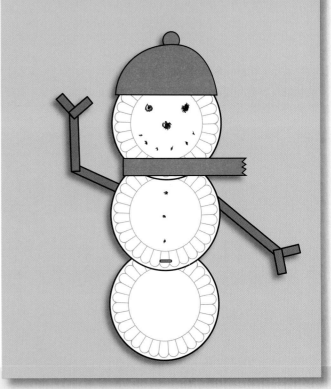

People Puppets
Dramatic expression
Encourage each child to decorate a plate so it resembles his face. Then help him tape a large craft stick to the back of the plate. Invite students to use the resulting puppets to act out stories.

Fancy Flowers
Fine-motor skills
Invite a child to color a plate so it resembles a flower. Then invite him to fringe-cut the edges of his plate and glue his plate to a construction paper stem. As a finishing touch, have him cut green paper leaves and glue them to the stem.

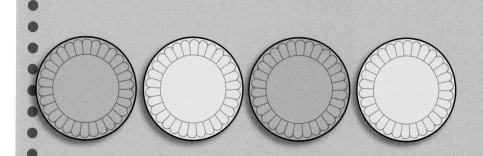

Serving Up Patterns
Creating patterns
Provide colorful paper plates. Have a child use the plates to make a simple *AB* pattern. After checking her pattern, encourage her to use the plates to create a different pattern.

Orderly Arrangement

Ordering numbers

Write each numeral from 1 to 10 on a separate paper plate. Arrange the plates in random order. Then invite a youngster to rearrange the plates to show the numbers in order.

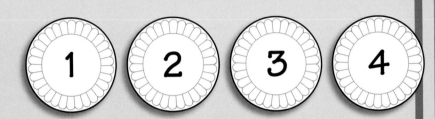

Super Stencils

Forming shapes

To make stencils, cut different shapes from heavy-duty paper plates. A child uses a variety of writing utensils to trace both the cutouts and the stencils on colorful paper.

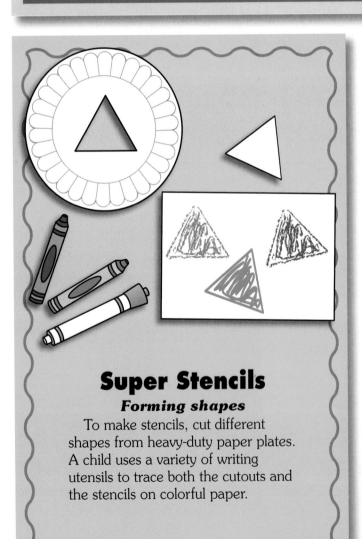

Halves to Wholes

Fractions

Cut several paper plates in half, using a different puzzle cut for each plate. Place the halves in a tub. Have a child lay out the halves and then put the puzzles together to make whole plates.

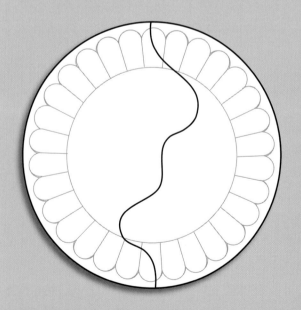

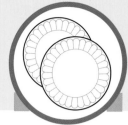

A Fun Frame
Fine-motor skills

Invite each child to decorate the edges of a white paper plate. Then have her punch a hole near the top of the plate and add a loop of ribbon for hanging. Encourage her to take the frame home and, with the help of her parents, attach a favorite photo.

All Kinds of Plates
Sorting

Place a collection of various plates in a tub. Invite a child to study the plates and then have him sort the plates into groups. Have him explain the sorting rule he used. Then encourage him to sort the plates using a different rule.

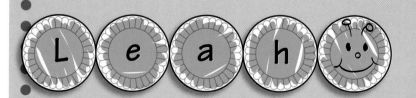

Namely, Caterpillars
Spelling one's name

Help each child write the letters in her name on separate paper plates. Prompt her to decorate them as desired. Then have her decorate an extra plate so it resembles a caterpillar head. Invite her to make a caterpillar by placing the head behind the plates arranged to spell her name.

Paper Towels

Double Dip
Mixing colors
Set out different colors of tinted water along with a supply of paper towel strips. Invite a child to dip a strip in one cup. Then encourage him to dip the strip in another cup. Have him name the resulting color at the end of his strip.

The Longest Roll
Comparing lengths
Place two partial paper towel rolls on the floor. Have youngsters predict which paper towel roll will be longer when it is unrolled. Then have a youngster stand on the first towel of each roll. Help youngsters unroll the paper towels and compare the result to their guess. Then have students separate and stack the paper towels for classroom use.

Strength Test
Observing, predicting
Have a volunteer hold a moist paper towel with both hands. Encourage youngsters to predict how many bear counters can be put on the towel before it tears. Then have students count aloud as they place bears on the towel. Encourage students to compare the final number to their predictions.

Lovely Rainbows
Fine-motor skills

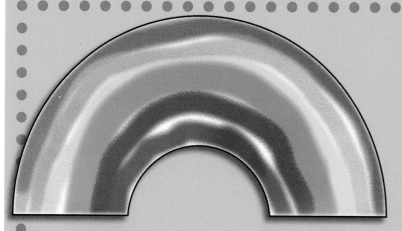

On a covered work surface, place rainbow shapes cut from sturdy white paper towels. A child uses washable markers to draw wide stripes on a cutout, leaving space between the stripes. Then she uses a paintbrush to brush water across the stripes. The colors will bleed into the spaces!

Water Race
Observing

Have two different youngsters attach clothespins to separate strips of paper towel. Encourage each child to grasp his clothespin and, on a signal, place the end of his strip in a cup of tinted water. Youngsters observe the paper towels until the water reaches the clothespin on one of the strips.

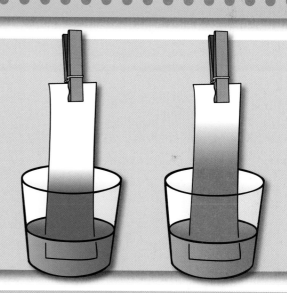

Soaking It Up
Investigating absorption

Provide a variety of paper items, such as paper towels, sandpaper, construction paper, and waxed paper. Have students predict which item would clean up a spill the best. Pour some water on a table. Then invite a volunteer to test each material. Lead students to understand that paper towels work best because they absorb water quickly.

Pattern Blocks

Fill It In
Completing a puzzle
On a sheet of tagboard, arrange pattern blocks to form a picture. Then trace around each block and place the blocks in a resealable plastic bag. Have a child remove each block from the bag and place it in an appropriate area on the tracing.

Measuring With Blocks
Nonstandard measurement
Set out a tub of pattern blocks along with several common classroom objects. Invite a child to choose an object and measure it by making a line of like pattern blocks next to the object. Then have her repeat the process with a different type of pattern block. Encourage her to compare the number of each type of block used.

Counting Sides
Sorting
Set out a small basket of pattern blocks along with three sheets of paper labeled as shown. Invite a child to take a block from the basket and count the number of sides it has. Then have her place it on the correct sheet of paper.

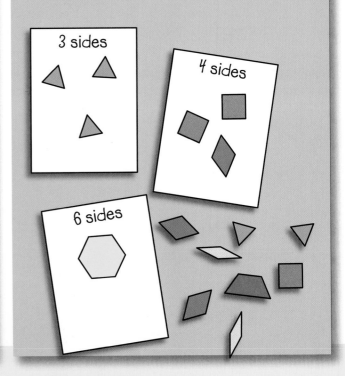

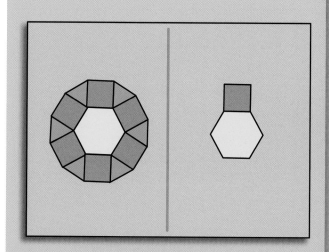

Dandy Designs
Spatial sense
For this partner activity, give each child a sheet of paper divided in half and access to pattern blocks. On one half of the paper, have him arrange pattern blocks to create a design. Then on the other side of the paper invite his partner to duplicate the design.

Keep It Going
Extending patterns
Arrange pattern blocks on tagboard strips to make patterns. Trace around the blocks and color in the tracings to make pattern starters. A child chooses a starter and then uses pattern blocks to extend the pattern.

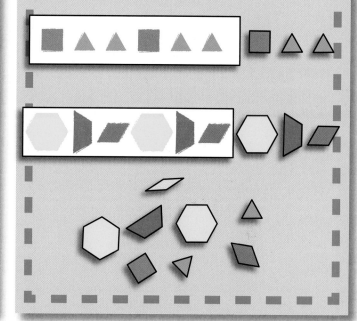

Covering Up
One-to-one correspondence
Prepare a gameboard similar to the one shown and make several copies. Give each player in a small group a gameboard. Provide a bag of pattern blocks. In turn, have each player take a block from the bag. Have him place the block on his board if it's needed. If the block is not needed, have him return the block to the bag. Play continues until one player covers his entire board.

Pipe Cleaners

Worm Pointers
Identifying colors

Wrap each of several colorful pipe cleaners around your finger to make a curl (worm) and then remove the pipe cleaner. Tell students that the worms enjoy eating only things that are the same colors they are. Have a child slide a worm on his finger and identify its color. Then encourage him to walk around the room, pointing to items that match the worm's color and saying, "Munch, munch, munch!"

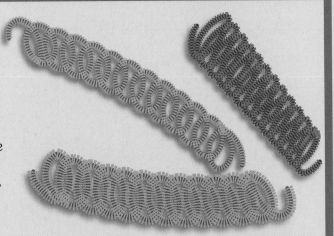

Line Up
Ordering by length

Set out several pipe cleaner pieces in varying lengths. Then have a child rearrange the pieces so they are in order from shortest to longest. After checking his work, encourage him to mix up the pipe cleaners and then rearrange them from longest to shortest.

Sandy Words
Writing, word recognition

Place colorful pipe cleaners and word cards near a sand tray. Have a child choose a pipe cleaner and a word card. Encourage him to read the word. Then invite him to use the pipe cleaner to write the word in the sand.

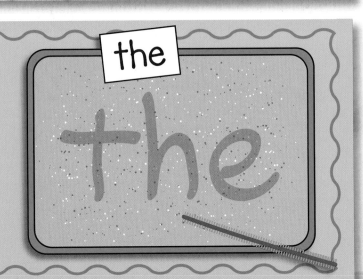

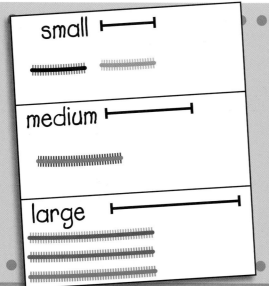

Just Right
Comparing length

Prepare a chart like the one shown. Place the chart near a basket of pipe cleaners cut to the corresponding lengths. A youngster chooses a pipe cleaner from the basket. Then he compares the pipe cleaner to each line on the chart and places it in the correct section.

Pipe Cleaner Pictures
Art

Set out a tub of colorful pipe cleaners in various lengths. Invite a child to arrange pipe cleaners on her paper to create a picture. Then have her glue the pipe cleaners in place.

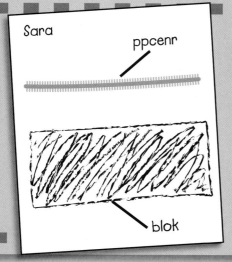

Matching Lengths
Writing

Give each child a length of pipe cleaner and invite her to find an object that is about the same length. Have her glue the pipe cleaner to a sheet of paper and then draw the object. Encourage her to label her drawing.

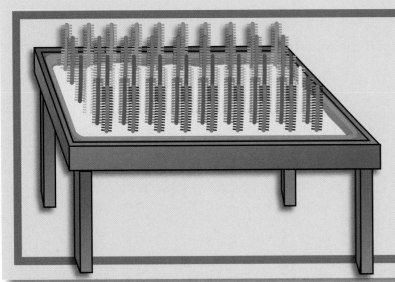

Planting a Rainbow
Sorting by color
Place colorful pipe cleaners near a sand table. Then invite a child to find all the pipe cleaners in one color and plant the pipe cleaners in a row. Encourage him to repeat the process with each remaining color.

Loopy Patterns
Creating patterns
Provide short lengths of pipe cleaner. Then have each child link pipe cleaners together to form a pattern. Finally, encourage her to read her pattern aloud.

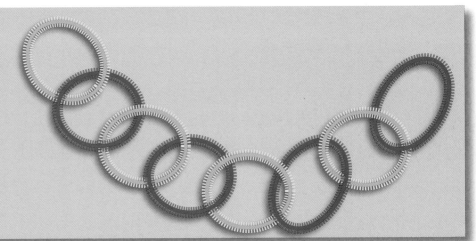

Name That Letter
Letter identification
Give each student pair several equal lengths of pipe cleaner. Have one partner use the pipe cleaners to form a letter. Then invite the other child to name the letter. Encourage students to switch roles and play another round.

Pipe Cleaners

Word Finder
Sight words

Bend several pipe cleaners as shown to form word finders. When reading with a student, give him the word finder and name a word. Then have him search the text for the word and highlight it using the word finder.

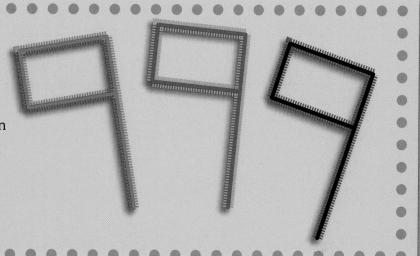

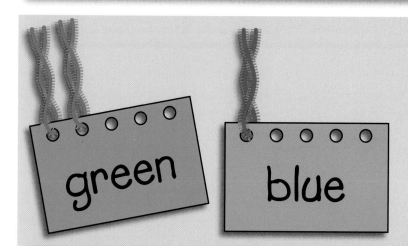

Colorful Words
Matching colors

Punch holes in color word cards and place the cards near pipe cleaners in matching colors. A youngster chooses a pipe cleaner and finds the matching card. Then he inserts the pipe cleaner into a hole in the card and twists it in place.

Squiggly Lines
Art

Place dollops of colorful paint on a sheet of paper. A youngster uses a paint roller or large paint brush to spread the paint over the paper. Then he uses a sturdy pipe cleaner to draw in the paint.

Swirls of Color
Exploring colors

For each child, squirt yellow, red, and blue paint in a resealable plastic bag. Help him seal the bag and then invite him to rub his fingers on the bag to swirl the colors together. After a few moments, have him stop and name the different colors he sees in the bag.

Air Bags
Investigating states of matter

Fill a plastic bag with air and then seal it. Gather a group of youngsters around the bag. Tell students that the bag is filled with air. To prove this, poke a small hole in the bag and, in turn, invite volunteers to hold their hands above the hole as you press on the bag. Encourage them to share what they feel.

Festive Beanbags
Gross-motor skills

Invite each child to fill a personalized plastic bag with colorful paper shreds and shiny confetti. Seal and tape the top of the bag. Store the bags until they are needed for use as game markers or for a tossing activity.

Writing in Paint
Letter recognition, letter formation
For each child, squirt a small amount of paint into a resealable plastic bag and then seal the bag. Write a letter on your board and have students name the letter. Then encourage each child to use his finger to write the letter on his bag.

Cookie Crumbs
Fine-motor skills
A child places two sandwich cookies in a plastic bag. She squeezes the bag to crumble the cookies. Then she opens the bag and sprinkles the crumbles over a cup of pudding. Finally, she enjoys her yummy snack!

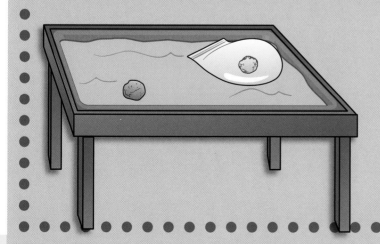

Flotation Question
Critical thinking
Place a rock in a plastic bag. Then fill the remaining area of the bag with air and seal it closed. Gather youngsters around a water table and place the prepared bag in the water as well as an individual rock. Invite youngsters to discuss why the rock in the bag floats but the other rock sinks.

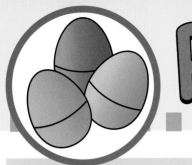

Plastic Eggs

Egg Toss
Gross-motor skills
Fill several eggs with rice and then secure them closed with packing tape. Place the eggs near a tape line on the floor and set a large basket a few feet away. Invite a child to stand on the line and toss each egg into the basket.

Putting It Together
Fine-motor skills
Separate a supply of eggs and place the halves in a container. Have a student remove the halves from the container. Then invite him to put matching halves together and place the whole eggs back in the container.

Tip the Scale
Comparing weight
Fill eggs with different materials, such as pennies, beans, or cotton balls. Then secure the eggs closed with packing tape. Invite a child to choose two eggs and place them on opposite sides of a balance scale to determine which egg is heavier. Have her repeat the process with other egg combinations.

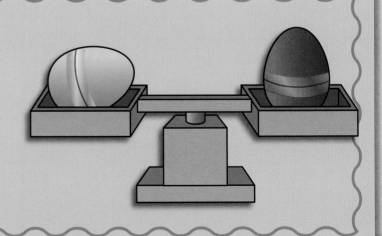

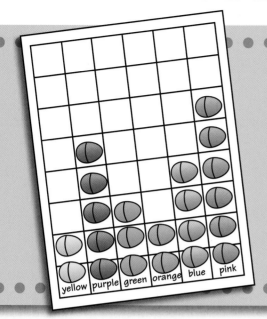

A Colorful Hunt
Graphing
Before little ones arrive, hide a supply of
eggs in the room. Invite youngsters to find the
eggs and place them on a floor graph similar to
the one shown. Then have students count and
compare the columns of eggs.

In the Bag
Counting
Write the numerals from 1
to 10 on separate paper bags.
Set the bags near a tub of eggs.
Invite a child to take a bag and
read the number. Then have
him place a matching number
of eggs in the bag.

Decorative Eggs
Art
Set out a class supply of eggs along with paper
scraps, glue, glitter, and pom-poms. Invite a child
to use the materials to decorate one of the eggs.
Then display his egg on a simple egg stand, such
as a personalized paper loop like the one shown.

Plastic Foods

Grocery Shopping
Visual memory

Gather several plastic food items and a paper grocery bag. Sit in a circle with your students. Show each food item to youngsters prior to placing it in the bag. Once all the food is in the bag, invite a volunteer to name one of the food items. Remove the item. Continue until each item has been removed.

Alike	Different
Both are yellow. Both are long.	A banana has a peel. Corn has kernels. A banana tastes good with ice cream.

Alike yet Different
Comparing

Label a simple chart as shown. Then display two food items. Invite youngsters to study the two items and name ways the items are alike and different. Write students' words on the chart.

Teacher's Lunch
Sense of touch

Write your name on a paper lunch bag and place a food item in the bag. Have each child reach into the bag and feel the item without looking in the bag. After each student has had a turn, invite volunteers to name the food item.

I think she has a chicken leg in her bag.

Ms. Jackson

This is a hamburger and hot dog sandwich.

Make a Sandwich

Letter-sound association

Give each youngster a plastic food item. Pretend to lay a large slice of bread down and then name a letter. Invite any student holding a food item whose name begins with that letter to say the food's name and add it to the silly sandwich. Finally, pretend to put another slice of bread atop the sandwich ingredients.

Food Clues

Critical thinking

Secretly show a child a food item. Then invite him to give his classmates clues about the food. After each clue, encourage him to choose a volunteer to guess the food item. Continue until the correct food is named.

Unpacking the Groceries

Sorting

On a sheet of poster board, draw a refrigerator. Then set grocery bags containing food items nearby. Have a student remove an item from a bag and place it on the refrigerator if it needs to remain cold. If the item does not need to remain cold, have him place it next to the refrigerator.

Play Dough

Sound Sculptures

Recognizing initial sounds

Name a letter and review its sound with students. Then have each youngster sculpt a ball of play dough into something that begins with the given letter. Encourage each child to share his sculpture with a classmate.

Shimmer and Shine

Forming and recognizing letters

Give each pair of students a ball of play dough mixed with glitter. Have one partner manipulate the dough to form a letter. Then have the remaining youngster name the letter. Have the pair switch roles and play another round.

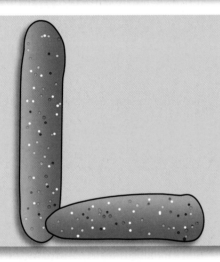

Birthday Cakes

Identifying numbers, making sets

Set out play dough, a set of number cards, and a supply of birthday candles. Have a child shape the dough to make a cake. Then invite him to take a number card and read the number. Encourage him to put a matching number of candles on the cake.

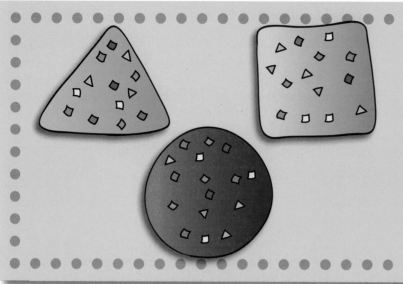

Shapes That Sparkle
Forming shapes

Mix shiny confetti in a batch of play dough. Give a child a ball of play dough and name a shape. Have him mold his play dough to form the named shape. After checking his work, repeat the activity with a different shape.

Play Dough Creatures
Classifying

Set out a variety of colorful play dough. Name animals from a specific geographic location, such as ocean animals. Invite a child to mold the dough to make several creatures from that area. Repeat the activity with animals from other locations, such as farm animals, forest animals, and jungle animals.

Ice Cream Creations
Listening

Place paper ice cream cones, disposable bowls, and an ice cream scoop near a supply of colorful play dough. Have youngsters use the props to pretend to order and make ice cream treats.

What's Inside?
Critical thinking
Secretly hide a small object, such as a toy car, inside a ball of play dough. Show youngsters the ball and give them a clue about the object inside. Invite a volunteer to name the object. Once the object has been identified, have youngsters help remove it from the play dough.

Slithering Along
Ordering by length
Have a child roll out several play dough snakes of different lengths. Then have her arrange the snakes in order from shortest to longest. After checking her work, invite her to order them from longest to shortest.

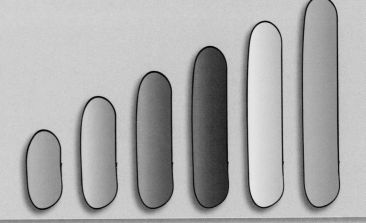

At the Restaurant
Dramatic expression
Set out several colors of play dough along with a variety of restaurant props. Have some youngsters pretend to be patrons while others pretend to be restaurant workers. Have the patrons order food and encourage the workers to use the play dough and other props to prepare and serve the food.

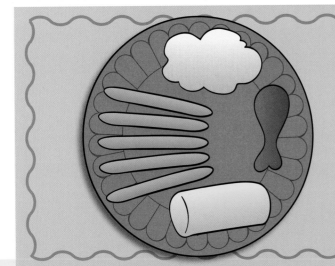

Play Dough

Veggie Soup
Fine-motor skills

Provide play dough, scissors, and a soup pot. A youngster forms the play dough into vegetable shapes. Then she uses the scissors to snip the play dough vegetables into small pieces to make a tasty pot of vegetable soup!

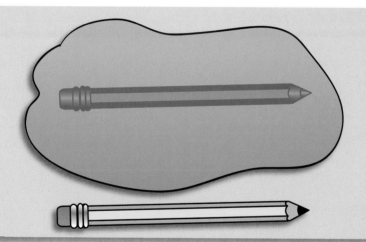

Make Your Mark
Visual discrimination

Place a batch of play dough near a collection of objects that will make distinct imprints. Have a youngster secretly press one of the objects into the play dough and then remove it. Invite another child to study the dough and choose the object used to make the imprint.

A Basket of Apples
Graphing

Have each child make a red, green, or yellow play dough apple and place it on a floor graph labeled as shown. After all the apples are on the graph, guide the youngsters in counting the apples in each column and comparing the columns of the graph.

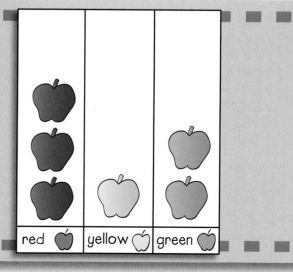

Pom-Poms

Critters on Location
Positional words

Have each child attach a pair of paper eyes to a large pom-pom. Then state a direction using a positional word, such as "Put your critter on your shoulder." After everyone has successfully followed the direction, announce a new direction for youngsters to follow.

Fluffy Words
Color words

Write a different color word on each of several large cards. Place the cards near a tub of corresponding pom-poms. Have a child take a card and read the word. Then invite him to cover the word with matching pom-poms.

More Peas, Please
Comparing sets

For this partner activity, set out a bowl of green pom-poms (peas), two large spoons, and two paper plates. Have each partner put a scoop of peas on her plate and count the peas. Then instruct the pair to compare the numbers. Invite the youngsters to return their peas to the bowl and play another round.

Picking Pumpkins
Fine-motor skills
Place a supply of orange pom-poms (pumpkins) on a sheet of brown paper (pumpkin patch). Set a pair of tweezers and a small basket nearby. A child uses the tweezers to "pick" each pumpkin and place it in the basket.

A Windy Race
Observing wind
Attach two parallel tape lines to your floor so they are several feet apart. Invite each of two players to place a pom-pom on a tape line. Have each child crouch behind his pom-pom. Then, at the signal, have each player blow on his pom-pom to move it across the finish line.

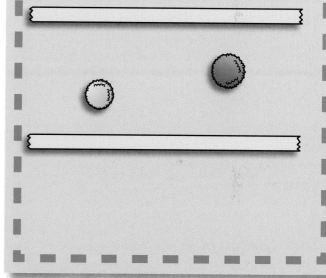

Fuzzy Soup
Sorting by color
Set out a large pot of colorful pom-poms and a ladle. A child removes a scoop of pom-poms from the pot and places them on a work surface. She sorts the pom-poms by color. Then she counts and compares each group.

Yummy Gumballs
Identifying numbers, making sets

Prepare a gumball machine cutout similar to the one shown. Place a set of number cards and a tub of pom-poms (gumballs) nearby. Invite a child to take a number card and read the number. Then have him place a matching set of gumballs on the machine.

Puffy Patterns
Extending patterns

Attach pom-poms to several tagboard strips to make patterns. Then set the strips near a tub of pom-poms. Invite a child to choose a strip and extend the pattern.

A Cloudy Day
Painting

A child dips a white pom-pom into a shallow pan of white paint. Then he makes cloud prints on a sheet of blue construction paper. When he is finished with his artwork, he counts the number of clouds.

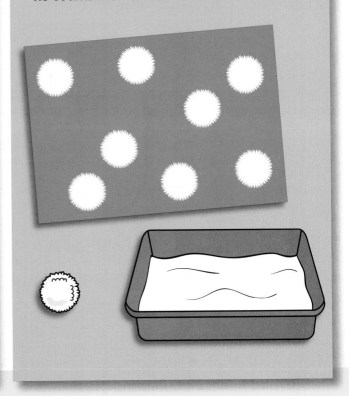

POM-POMS

Which Cup?
Ordinal numbers

Arrange disposable cups upside down in a row. Place a pom-pom critter under one of the cups. Slide the cups around to rearrange their order. Then invite a volunteer to use an ordinal number to name the cup he believes is concealing the critter. Lift the cup to show students whether the critter is under the cup. Continue until the correct cup is named.

Dozens of Eggs
Estimation, one-to-one correspondence

Put a few dozen large white pom-poms (eggs) in a basket. Place the basket near several sterilized egg cartons. Invite a youngster to estimate how many cartons the eggs will fill. Then have her place the eggs in the cartons. Encourage her to compare her estimate to the actual number of cartons used.

Two by Two
Making pairs

Divide a paper strip into ten sections and set a basket of pom-poms nearby. Invite a child to place a pair of pom-poms on each section of the strip. Then have him count the number of pairs he made. For an added challenge, encourage the child to count the pom-poms by twos.

Puppets

Hungry Harry
Initial sounds

Gather picture cards, including several with items that begin with /h/. Introduce a puppet as Harry and explain that it only eats things that begin with /h/. Invite a volunteer to take a card and name the picture. If the picture's name begins with /h/, have the child feed the card to Harry. If it does not, have him set the card aside.

Pass the Plate
Fine-motor skills

Have students sit in a circle, and invite each child to don a puppet. Then put a paper plate in the mouth of one puppet. Instruct youngsters to pass the plate around the circle using only their puppets' mouths.

I Can Handle It
Role-playing

For this activity, give a pair of students each a puppet. Describe a scenario to the class and encourage the pair to use the puppets to act out an inappropriate way to handle the situation. Then invite another pair of students to use the puppets to act out a good way to handle the situation.

Oh, I must have left it in the room with all the books.

On a Search
Listening

Hide an object in a location outside your classroom. Then use a puppet to tell the class that the object is lost and that the puppet needs your little ones' help to find it. Use the puppet to give clues about the object's location. Help youngsters follow the clues until they find the lost object.

Tell Us a Story
Recognizing story details

After reading a story, use a puppet to retell the story with a few errors. Encourage youngsters to politely stop and correct the puppet when there is a mistake.

Detective Puppet
Observation skills

Decorate a puppet so it resembles a detective. Each day, prior to dismissal, invite a youngster to wear the puppet and to check whether every area in the room has been cleaned up. Have the youngster use the puppet to report his findings.

Puzzle Pieces

Let's Trace!
Fine-motor skills
Gather a variety of wooden puzzle pieces with handles. A child places a puzzle piece on a sheet of paper and traces it. He repeats the process with other puzzle pieces, overlapping the tracings as desired. Then he colors his artwork.

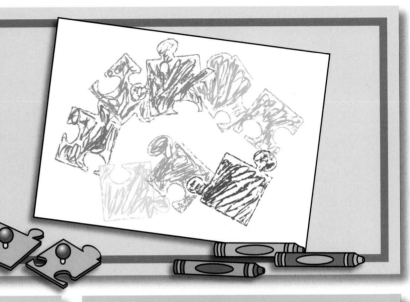

P Is for Puzzle
Forming the letter P
Make a large letter *P* card for each child. Have him trace the letter with his finger and say the letter's name. Then help him understand that the word *puzzle* begins with the letter *P*. Encourage him to glue colorful puzzle pieces to the letter. When the glue is dry, have him once again trace the letter with his finger and say its name.

Blue

Not Blue

Is It Blue?
Sorting
Place a variety of puzzle pieces at a table along with two plastic containers labeled as shown. A child selects a puzzle piece and looks to see whether any portion of it is the chosen color. Then she places it in the correct container. She continues with the remaining puzzle pieces.

GLUE

Fabulous Fall Tree

Investigating the seasons

Have youngsters paint puzzle pieces a variety of fall-related colors. Allow the pieces to dry. Then encourage students to draw a tree trunk on a sheet of construction paper. Have students glue the puzzle pieces above the trunk so they resemble colorful fall leaves.

Crackers for Quackers

Counting

Place a blue sheet of paper on the floor so it resembles a pond. Then place duck cutouts on the pond. Provide a container of puzzle pieces (crackers). A child rolls a die and counts the dots. Then she counts out a matching number of crackers and tosses them to the ducks.

Terrific Texture

Investigating the sense of touch

Glue puzzle pieces to a piece of cardboard and then attach the cardboard to a tabletop. A youngster feels the texture of the pieces. Then he places a piece of paper over the pieces and rubs the side of a crayon over the paper.

Rhythm Instruments

Watch and Play
Observation skills

Give each child a rhythm instrument and have youngsters sit in groups based on their instruments. Play an upbeat musical recording and have students watch you carefully. Throughout the recording, point to separate groups of youngsters, encouraging them to play along with the music. Whenever you point to a new group, the group that was playing previously stops playing until they are pointed to again.

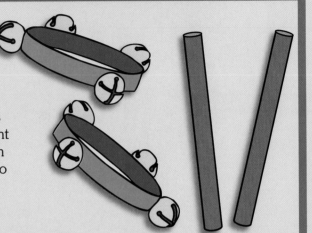

Echo Playing
Listening skills

Play a simple *AB* pattern with your rhythm instrument, such as tapping your knees and then your hand. Then prompt youngsters to repeat the pattern with their own instruments. When students are comfortable with this game, have them repeat *ABB* or *ABC* patterns.

Tap the Words
Phonological awareness

Choose a simple picture book with short sentences. After several readings of the book, give each child a rhythm instrument. Read a sentence from the book. Then, as you read it again, have students tap their instruments once for each word. For more advanced students, have them identify the number of words in the sentence. Continue with several other sentences from the book.

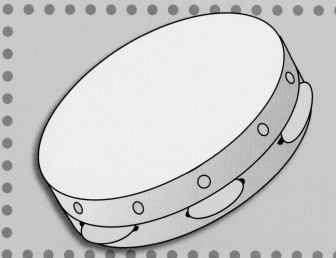

Hand, Elbow, Head
Identifying body parts

Hand each youngster a tambourine and then tell him to tap the tambourine against the palm of his hand. After several taps, encourage each youngster to tap his instrument against his elbow. Repeat the process, changing body parts to include head, knees, feet, ankles, shoulders, fingers, stomachs, and hips.

Little Lost Dog
Listening skills

Choose a child to be the seeker and give each remaining child a rhythm instrument. While the seeker closes her eyes, hide a dog cutout in the room. Have the seeker open her eyes and then walk slowly about the room, searching for the hidden dog. As she walks, prompt youngsters to play their instruments quietly when the seeker is far away from the dog and loudly when she is near the dog. When the child finds the dog, play another round of the game.

Follow the Beat
Gross-motor skills

Tap a rhythm instrument with a slow, steady beat and encourage youngsters to move to the beat. Continue tapping the instrument, changing the tempo and prompting students to move faster or slower accordingly.

Rubber Stamps

Simple Headbands
Patterning

Have each child stamp a pattern onto a sentence strip. (If desired, provide a prestamped strip for the student to copy.) Then size the strip to fit the child's head and staple the strip accordingly. For added interest, use stamps related to your current classroom theme.

That's My Name!
Spelling one's own name

Place alphabet stamps at a table along with an ink pad, a ring of student name cards, and paper. A child flips through the ring and finds his own name. Then he stamps his name onto a sheet of paper. If desired, he also stamps his classmates' names.

Festive Streamers
Fine-motor skills

Provide stamps related to the current season. Then have youngsters stamp images on lengths of adding machine tape as desired. Help them staple their tape pieces to the ends of cardboard tubes. Then prompt youngsters to shake the resulting streamers to a seasonal song!

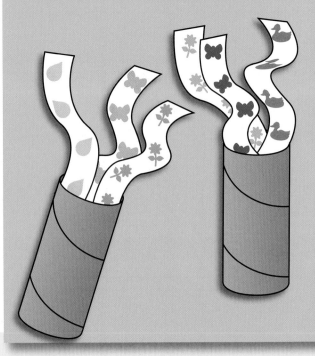

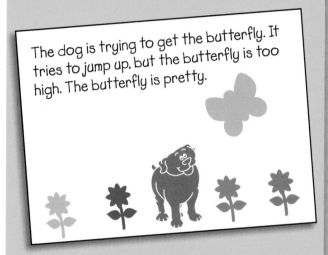

The dog is trying to get the butterfly. It tries to jump up, but the butterfly is too high. The butterfly is pretty.

Stamp Stories
Writing
Have a child stamp a variety of images onto a sheet of paper. Then encourage the child to tell a story about the picture he made as you write his words on the paper.

Letter Strips
Alphabetical order
Stamp the alphabet on a length of adding machine tape and attach it to a table. Place the letter stamps at a table along with an ink pad and blank strips of adding machine tape. A child points to the letters on the prestamped strip as he sings the alphabet song. Then he stamps the letters on a blank strip in alphabetical order, using the attached strip as a reference if needed.

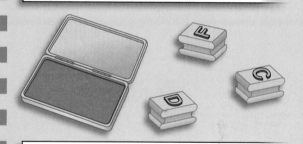

A B C D E F G H I

A B C

Shooting Stars
Art
A child presses a star stamp in a metallic silver stamp pad. Then he stamps star images on a sheet of black paper. Next, he presses his finger in the ink and makes streaks beside each star.

Sandy Stamps

Fine-motor skills

Provide a tub of moist sand and several simple rubber stamps. A child presses the stamps in the moist sand, making an impression. When the sand's surface is covered with impressions, he pats the sand so it's smooth and then repeats the process.

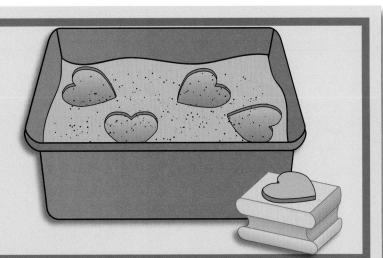

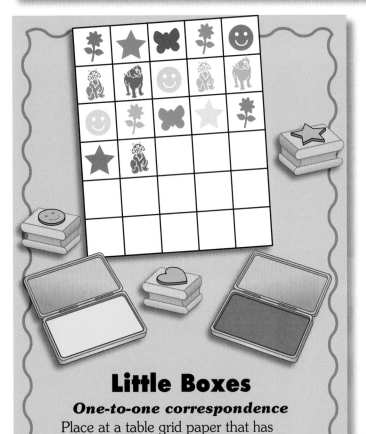

Little Boxes

One-to-one correspondence

Place at a table grid paper that has large boxes. Also provide small stamps and ink pads. A child develops one-to-one correspondence by stamping an image in each box.

At the Store

Identifying coins

Place coin stamps, ink pads, paper, and scissors at your grocery store center. A youngster stamps and identifies the coins. Then he cuts them out to use when pretending to purchase goods.

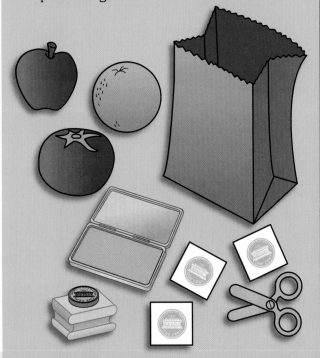

Rubber Stamps

Making Groups
Categorizing
Fold a sheet of paper in half for each child and label the halves as shown. A child stamps images of living things and nonliving things under the appropriate headings.

Time to Count
Identifying numbers, counting
Give a child a set of large number cards similar to the ones shown. She chooses a card and identifies the number. Then she stamps the appropriate number of images on the card. She repeats the process for each remaining card.

Make a Face
Art
Place geometric rubber stamps at a table along with colorful ink pads. Provide paper programmed with large circles. A youngster stamps colorful shapes on a circle to create a face.

Sponges

Rectangle, Oval, Rectangle, Oval

Patterning

Place two different-shaped sponges at a table along with a length of paper and a shallow container of paint. A child presses the sponges in the paint and then makes prints on the paper to form a pattern.

Sponge Science

Investigating sinking and floating

Put sponges in your water table. Encourage each student to visit the table and put a dry sponge in the water, noting that it floats. Have her saturate the sponge with water to make it sink. Then prompt her to squeeze all the water out of the sponge to make it float again!

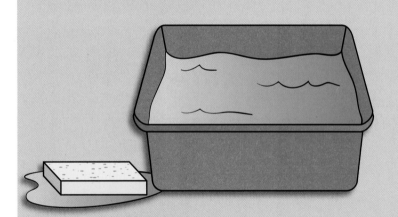

Fabulous Fish

Art

Have each youngster make sponge prints on a large sheet of light blue paper. When the paint is dry, encourage him to add details to the sponge prints to create lovely fish and then add details to complete the underwater scene.

Build It Up!
Spatial skills
Provide a variety of large car-washing sponges in your block area. Encourage students to use these soft building blocks in their constructions.

Soft Toss
Gross-motor skills
Place a tape line on the floor in a traffic-free area of the classroom. Put a container of sponges next to the tape line and then place a bucket several feet away. A child stands on the tape line and tosses sponges into the bucket.

Water Writing
Forming letters
Gather sponges and place them near your chalkboard along with a container of water. A child dips a sponge in the water and partially rings it out. Then he uses the sponge to draw letters on the board. When the letters disappear, he repeats the process.

Squeeze!
Fine-motor skills
Give each child a sponge and play a recording of upbeat music. Prompt youngsters to squeeze the sponge to the beat, changing hands halfway through the song.

Washing the Dishes
Art
Gather a variety of dishwashing sponges with handles. Place them in your art area along with paper plates and shallow containers of paint. A child dips the sponge in the paint and then swirls it on a plate as if washing the plate. He repeats the process with other colors of paint.

Nice and Clean
Gross-motor skills
Place containers with small amounts of soapy water around the room and give each child a sponge. Encourage him to dip his sponge in the water. Then have him use the sponge to bend and stretch to scrub chairs, tables, and other appropriate furniture.

Sponges

Beautiful Bugs
Investigating living things

Gather sponges and trim them as needed to make the shapes shown. Have a student make prints with the sponges so the prints resemble a head, a thorax, an abdomen, and wings. When the paint is dry, encourage him to use a marker to add details to his insect.

Make a Match
Matching letters

Gather several letter-shaped sponges and trace them on a sheet of paper. Laminate the paper and place the sponges in a tub of water. A child wrings out a sponge and then places it over the appropriate tracing.

Bath Time!
Recognizing body parts

Give each youngster a sponge and play a recording of upbeat music. Say, "Wash your arm!" Then prompt each child to dance as he "washes" his arm with the sponge. Continue calling out different body parts, such as hands, shoulders, legs, knees, stomach, and ankles.

Stencils

Make a Collage
Art
Provide a variety of stencils at a table. A child traces the stencils onto a sheet of paper, overlapping the stencils as desired. Then she colors her artwork.

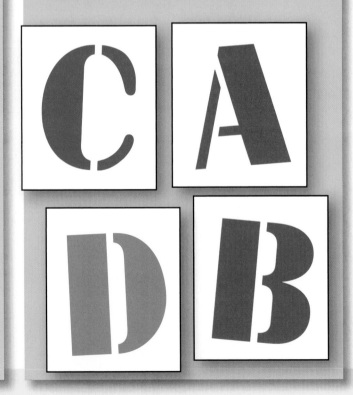

Letter Cards
Identifying letters
Place letter stencils at a table along with blank index cards. A child traces a stencil on a card and colors it in. Then he identifies the letter. He continues in the same way to make his own set of letter cards.

Trace the Number
Counting, identifying numbers
Place number stencils at a table along with paper and sets of manipulatives. A child chooses a number stencil. She traces it on a sheet of paper and colors it in. Then she counts the appropriate number of manipulatives and places them on the paper.

Letter and Number Sort
Sorting

Place letter and number stencils in a basket. A child removes the stencils from the basket and sorts them into two piles.

Make a Match
Matching letters

Trace letter stencils on a sheet of chart paper and color them in to make the alphabet. Place the letter stencils in a gift bag. Then have a child take a stencil and place it over the corresponding letter on the paper. Continue with each remaining letter.

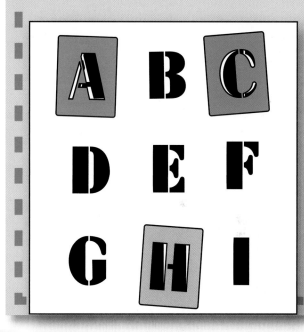

Marvelous Mural
Fine-motor skills

Attach a length of bulletin board paper to a table and provide a variety of stencils related to a specific theme. Encourage youngsters to visit the table and trace stencils on the paper. Then have them color the stencils as desired. Mount the finished artwork on a wall.

Critter Creations
Drawing

On a sheet of paper, have a child draw an outdoor scene. Then invite him to attach one or more sticky dots to his drawing. Encourage him to add details to the dots to make bugs.

In a Line
Number order

Give each child a paper strip and ten sticky dots with the backing still intact. Help her write the numbers 1 through 10 on the sticky dots. Then have her attach the dots to the paper strip in order.

Hopping Along
Counting

For this partner game, affix an equal line of sticky dots to each of two long paper strips. Place the strips near two small plastic animals and a die. In turn, have each player roll the die and make his animal hop a matching number of spaces. Play continues until one child reaches the end of his strip.

Connect the Dots
Fine-motor skills

On a sheet of paper, arrange numbered sticky dots so they form a shape when lines are drawn to connect them in order. Draw a line to connect the last dot to the first and then slip the paper into a plastic sheet protector. A child uses a dry-erase marker to connect the dots.

Go and Stop
Gross-motor skills

Draw several paths on a length of bulletin board paper. Attach a green sticky dot at the beginning of each path and a red dot at the end. Then have a child move a toy car along each path from the green dot to the red dot.

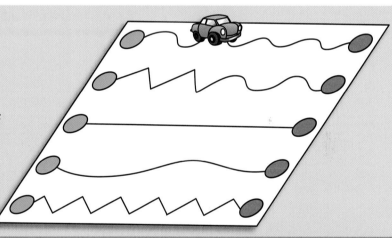

Color Coded
Sorting

Have each child attach a colorful sticky dot to her shirt. Then invite youngsters to sort themselves into groups based on the colors of their sticky dots. Encourage students in each group to name a few classroom objects that match their color.

Noted Names

Spelling one's own name

Give each child a number of sticky notes equal to the number of letters in her name. Then help her write one letter of her name on each note and arrange the notes in a random order. Encourage her to rearrange the letters to spell her name.

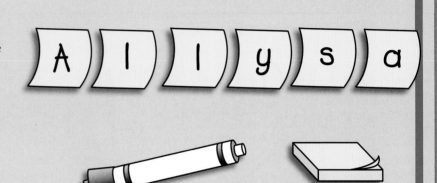

Sound Search

Letter-sound association

Write a letter on a sticky note. Give the note to a child and review the letter's sound. Then invite him to find an object that begins with the same letter and attach his note to the object.

Where Is Smiley?

Number recognition

While students are not looking, draw a smiley face on the board. Then place numbered sticky notes on the board, covering the smiley face with one note. Invite a volunteer to name a number and remove the note. Play continues until the face is revealed.

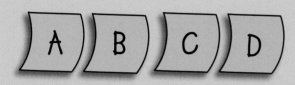

Letters in a Row
Alphabetical order
Program each of 26 sticky notes with a different letter. Distribute the notes among the students. Have the student with *A* on his note place it on the board. Invite students to continue in this manner until the alphabet is posted in order.

Our Preferences
Graphing
On a board, draw a graph similar to the one shown. Have each child write his name on a sticky note. Then invite him to post his note on the graph to mark his preference. After the graph is complete, encourage youngsters to discuss the results.

Favorite Pets

Lori		
Tina	Kim	Kelly
Dog	Cat	Other

Sticky Puzzles
Completing a puzzle
Arrange four sticky notes on a flat surface and draw a shape on the notes. Repeat the process with other sets of four and different shapes. Randomly place the notes on a board. A child arranges the sets to reveal the shapes.

Tape

Letter Moves

Letter recognition, gross-motor skills

Affix masking tape to the floor to form a large *T.* Then invite youngsters to tiptoe on the *T.* Repeat the activity with other letters and actions, such as *H* for hop, *J* for jump, *M* for march, or *W* for waddle.

A Colorful Collection

Sorting by color

Use masking tape to divide a table into a desired number of sections and place a different-colored card in each section. Then set a tub of objects with corresponding colors near the table. Have a child sort the objects onto the correct sections of the table.

Musical Shapes

Shape recognition

Affix tape to the floor to make several large shapes. Play lively music and invite youngsters to move around the area. Stop the music and name a shape. Then encourage students to quickly stand in the appropriate shape.

Make a Print
Exploring fingerprints
Rub a sheet of paper with the side of a pencil's point. To make a fingerprint, a child presses a fingertip on the rubbing. He places a piece of transparent tape on his fingertip and gently removes the tape. Then he attaches it to a personalized index card. Encourage him to use a magnifying glass to study his fingerprint.

How Long?
Nonstandard measurement
Attach different lengths of colorful tape to a sheet of paper. Place the paper near a tub of linking cubes. Have a youngster use the cubes to measure each length of tape.

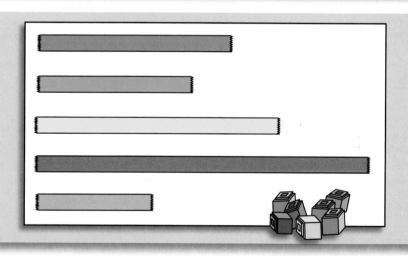

On the Tightrope
Balancing
Attach a line of masking tape to the floor to make a tightrope. Have a child balance a beanbag on her head while she carefully walks across the tightrope. Prompt her to repeat the activity, walking forward, backward, and sideways.

Toy Vehicles

Watch the Road!
Gross-motor skills

Draw a road on a piece of black bulletin board paper. Then place several objects on the road to represent obstacles. A child maneuvers a toy car down the road, being careful not to hit the obstacles.

Sidewalk Driving
Working cooperatively

For this outdoor activity, gather a class supply of toy vehicles and sidewalk chalk. On a sidewalk, encourage youngsters to work together to draw roads, houses, and other buildings. Then invite them to drive the vehicles on the roads.

Parking Lot
Identifying letters

On a sheet of paper draw a parking lot like the one shown and make a copy for each child. Give each child a parking lot and a toy vehicle. Name a letter or a sound and have her park her vehicle in the matching space. Repeat the process several times, having her move her car each time.

In the Garage
Sorting

Sort two groups of vehicles into separate plastic containers (garages). Then invite youngsters to explain how the vehicles are sorted. Encourage volunteers to suggest other ways to sort the vehicles. Enlist students' help in sorting the vehicles using the suggestions.

An Adventurous Trip
Oral language

Obtain a toy bus and sit in a circle with your youngsters. Begin an exciting story about a class trip. Pass the bus to the child beside you and encourage him to add to the story. Continue until each child has had a turn.

Traffic Jam
Comparing sets

Prepare two roads like the ones shown and place a few toy vehicles on each road. Encourage youngsters to use words such as *more, less*, and *equal* to compare the numbers of vehicles on the roads.

Building Roads

Gross-motor skills

Set a container of toy vehicles near your block area. Invite youngsters to use the blocks to build a road system. Then encourage youngsters to drive the vehicles on the roads.

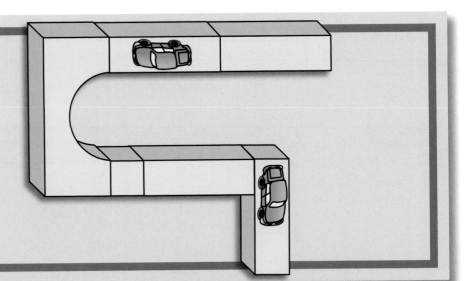

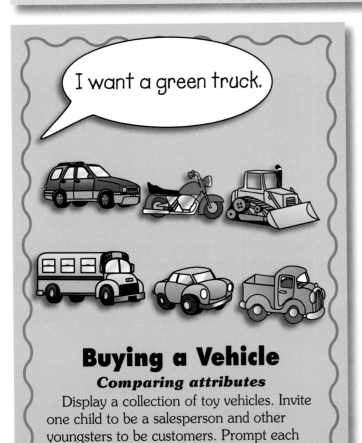

Buying a Vehicle

Comparing attributes

Display a collection of toy vehicles. Invite one child to be a salesperson and other youngsters to be customers. Prompt each customer to use two attributes to describe the vehicle she wishes to purchase. The salesperson searches his selection and gives the customer a matching vehicle.

Taking a Road Trip

Speaking

For this version of Hot Potato, invite youngsters to pass a toy car around the circle as music plays. Stop the music and encourage the youngster holding the car to name a place she would like to visit during a road trip.

Zoom!
Identifying and forming shapes
Provide toy vehicles and a set of supersize shape cards. Invite a youngster to choose a card and name the shape. Then have him "drive" a car around the perimeter of the shape.

Artistic Tracks
Art
Place toy vehicles in shallow containers of paint. Have a youngster repeatedly roll the vehicles across a sheet of paper to make tracks.

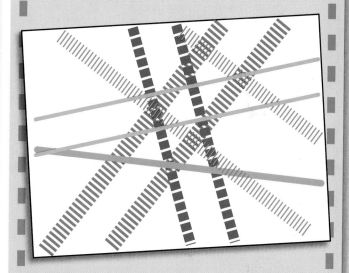

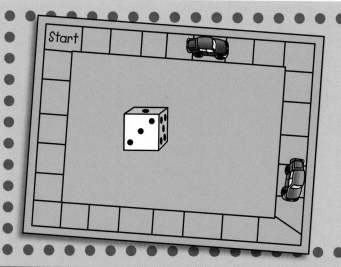

On the Move
Counting
To prepare for this partner game, make a gameboard like the one shown. To play, have each child roll a die in turn. He uses a toy vehicle as a game marker and moves the number of spaces indicated on the die. Play continues until a player moves around the entire gameboard.

 Yarn

Listen and Do
Positional words
Give each youngster a length of yarn and encourage him to place it on the floor to form a circle. Then give a direction such as "Stand inside your circle." Continue giving other directions using positional words.

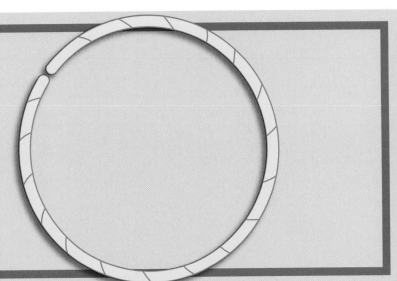

Yummy Spaghetti
Sorting by length
Provide a bowl of yarn pieces (spaghetti) in two different lengths. Place the bowl near two paper plates labeled as shown. Invite your little chefs to sort the spaghetti onto the two plates.

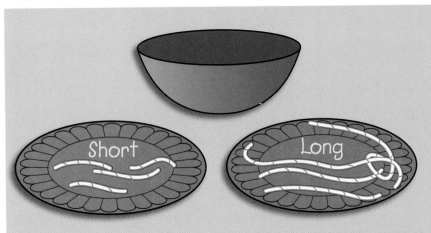

Short

Long

Dip and Drag
Art
A child dips a piece of yarn into a shallow pan of paint and then drags the yarn across a sheet of paper. He repeats the process with other colors of paint.

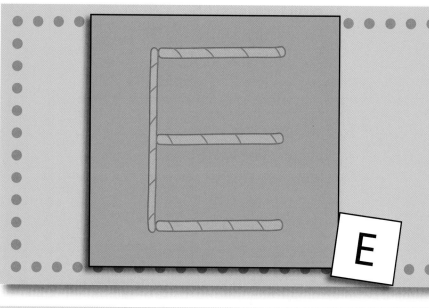

Sticky Letters
Letter recognition and formation
Place a set of letter cards and various lengths of yarn pieces near a flannelboard. Invite a child to take a card and name the letter. Then have her use the yarn pieces to form the letter on the flannelboard.

Looking for Worms
Counting
Bury lengths of yarn (worms) in a sand table and place a pair of tweezers nearby. Invite a youngster to use the tweezers to remove the worms from the sand. Then have him count the number of worms he found.

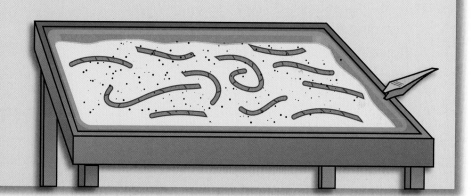

Slithering Snakes
Comparing lengths
Give each youngster several yarn pieces of different lengths (snakes). Then, on a sheet of paper, have her order the snakes from shortest to longest. After checking her work, invite her to glue the snakes to her paper.

Skills Index

Literacy

Math